The Art of Talking to Yourself

Self-Awareness Meets the Inner Conversation

VIRONIKA TUGALEVA

Soulux Press

A publication of SOULUX PRESS.

The purpose of this book is to provide inspiration and present a helpful viewpoint. The publisher and author do not accept legal responsibility for the misuse of its contents.

To connect with the author, visit www.vironika.org.

Cover design by Amelia Mirón Castro.

Midnight Constellations font by Shara Weber.

LIBRARY AND ARCHIVES CANADA CATALOGUING IN PUBLICATION DATA

Tugaleva, Vironika, 1988-, author

The art of talking to yourself : self-awareness meets the inner conversation / Vironika Tugaleva.

Issued in print and electronic formats.

ISBN   978-0-9920468-3-5   (softcover).--ISBN   978-0-9920468-4-2 (HTML)

1. Self-realization.   I. Title.

BF637.S4T84 2017   158.1   C2017-900247-3

                                                     C2017-900248-1

I dedicate this book to the truth seekers of the world—those who insist on searching for what is real even when it's painful, inconvenient, and tiresome. You give me hope.

You've no idea how hard I've looked for a gift to bring You.
Nothing seemed right.
What's the point of bringing gold to the gold mine, or water to the Ocean.
Everything I came up with was like taking spices to the Orient.
It's no good giving my heart and my soul because you already have these.
So I've brought you a mirror.
Look at yourself and remember me.

RUMI

Table of Contents

Acknowledgements

✖ ✖ ✖ ✖ ✖ ✖ ✖ ✖

I began writing this book shortly after I wrote my first. The early drafts, however, bear little resemblance to what you have in your hands today. *The Art of Talking to Yourself* began as yet another self-help book written by yet another "expert." In the four years I spent writing this manuscript, I gained new eyes. The changes that have taken place, within me as well as my work, would not have been possible without the people who stood by my side.

I am eternally grateful to my clients of past and present. You have allowed me into the deepest woods of your minds. There, I have learned about human nature. And I have learned so much about myself from your trust and feedback. I especially want to thank Lorissa for showing me the value and importance of friendship; Barbara, for your open mind and wild spirit; Roxana, for being vulnerable even when it was hard; Stephanie, for always telling me the whole truth and nothing but; Debbi, for showing me how gentleness and strength can coexist without diluting one another; Mel, for your sense of humour; Karen, for your unequivocal trust; Latoya, for your playfulness and forgiveness; Madison, for your creativity and curiosity; Wendi, for your gentle wisdom and patience; Brian, for your open mind and big heart; and Molly, for showing me all your colours and helping me liberate my own.

I am grateful to the authors at *The Real Us* as well as the administrators and members of the *Love Tribes*. You have inspired me with your courage, tenacity, and honesty. I am grateful to all my readers and followers. Thank you for allowing my words into your hearts, trusting me with your stories, and reminding me that my voice matters. You have given me strength and courage. You have held me to a higher standard of being. You have shared my joy and my pain. You keep me going, even when it's hard.

Amelia, you have helped me more than I could have ever imagined. You have sprinkled my life with many acts of kindness—each an unexpected, heartwarming surprise. I couldn't have found a more suitable designer for the cover of this book. You make beautiful art, and you are a beautiful person. I hope that our journey together will continue for many years to come.

Lei, you have not only helped me edit this book, but you have also held space for my painful creative process. Thank you for laughing along with me at all the strange stories woven by my well-intentioned mind. I appreciate your sense of humour and compassion. This journey would not have been half as enjoyable without you.

Thank you, Lori, for being my mentor and my friend. As a mentor, you have taught me about vulnerability, leadership, and community building. As a friend, you've shown me true reciprocity, and you've given me a safe space to exist, speak, and feel seen. I wouldn't trade our conversations for anything.

Thank you, Ken, for your drive, honesty, and tenacity. Your creative passion has inspired my own, and you have taught me the importance of churning criticism into inspired action. Thank you, Joanna, for our long conversations and your excitement about this book.

I am also grateful for the few friends who have stayed close to me throughout the past decade: Alisha, Marc, Alanna, Nicole, and Theo. It's more than a little magical that you've stuck with me through all my seasons. With each year, our memories become a little more meaningful, our bonds a bit more irreplaceable.

Thank you, mom, for being a fan of my writing since the early days. Thank you, dad, for putting all those philosophical questions into my mind as a child. It made a difference. Thank you both for working so hard to leave the Ukraine and make a better life for us. If not for your courage, hard work, and persistence, I wouldn't be writing this book. I'm sorry it took me so long to feel this gratitude.

Maryna, thank you for believing in my potential and my beauty, even when I didn't. Thank you, Zoya, for being such a nurturing, caring presence in my life; Kolya, for your trust and your big smile; Misha, for telling me all those stories when I was young and planting within me the seeds of creativity; and Ivan, for your sense of humour and your honesty. Thank you, Jackie, for being a role model of unconditional love and kindness; David, for having the best stories and never hesitating to do me a favour; Rebecca and Dave, for all our laughs; Lianne, for your generosity; and Kieran, for your optimism.

My final thank you is bound to be inadequate. In my years of trying to make a difference in the world, I have faced as much light as darkness. When I have fallen into deep holes within my psyche, I have often logged out of the digital world where many of my friends and supporters gather. In those times, you've always been there, Jamie. You've seen the beautiful mess that I am, and you've not only accepted that mess into your heart, but you've also taught me to accept it deeper than I ever thought possible. I'm grateful for your support. And I'm even more grateful for the space we both work so hard to build together: a safe haven where we can both feel seen and understood. Even when it feels impossible, we keep trying. Constructing this emotional sanctuary with you—however difficult it has been—has taught me to do the same with other people. Our journey has given me hope for a more intimate, compassionate, and connected world. Our relationship has made me a better coach, better friend, and better human being. You've taught me to listen. You've helped me dispel my idealisms and fears about being intimate with another person. And, together, we've searched for a deeper truth beyond what our childhoods and societies taught us. We've been mirrors for each other's experience. That has simultaneously been the most painful and most beautiful thing. You were the first paradox I ever loved, and you've made me who I am today. There aren't enough words to thank you. But as you read this book, you will find pieces of me, pieces of yourself, and pieces of what we've discovered together. As much as this is a story of my understanding and a story of the human condition, it is also the story of us.

Introduction

✳ ✳ ✳ ✳ ✳ ✳ ✳

In my early days of writing this book, a friend asked me what I was writing about. I said something like "self-awareness and the dangers of self-help." He looked confused.

"In the past few years," I explained, "I've met a shocking number of people who blindly trust self-help experts and their advice. They don't think they know any better. I'm hoping this book can be different. Instead of playing guru and giving advice, I want to encourage people to be self-aware and trust themselves."

"So..." he paused, "you're writing ...a self-help book ...about ...how people shouldn't trust self-help books?"

"Yes," I laughed. "I suppose I am."

Another friend suggested that this book's opening line should say, "I am an expert in knowing experts aren't experts." One of my beta readers joked that I am "a bit like a turkey voting for Thanksgiving." As this book spreads, I am sure it will seem strange to many people. I admit that it *is* strange, ironic, and maybe even hypocritical, but not impossible and certainly not useless.

I do have a not-so-secret hope that one day this book will be part of a new "Self-Discovery" section. These books would point you toward the helping hand that you're already extending to yourself (instead of giving you miracle tactics under studied or blessed authority). At the time of

1

my writing this, only the "Self-Help" section exists. But I do not mean to blame my hypocrisy on the developed world's book classification system. If anyone is to blame (or thank, I suppose, depending on your perspective), it is me. I just couldn't keep my hand out of the cookie jar.

In my first book, *The Love Mindset*, I wrote about the lessons I learned after my ten-year struggle with addiction, eating disorders, and self-hatred almost culminated in suicide. At the time, I thought I was having a mental breakdown. It turned out to be (or, you could say, I reframed it as) an awakening. I could have kept that story to myself. How many people experience mental breakdowns each year? Each month? Each moment? How many people grow up, heal their insecurities, and grow into their potential? I have met thousands of such people over the past few years. And how many of them choose to share what they've learned with the world? Compare that to the far larger number of people who choose to keep their experiences private.

It was not the discovery of love that first compelled me to write *The Love Mindset*. It was neither my struggle nor my healing that first inspired me to coach people through their struggles and healing. It was self-help.

A few months before I had read my first self-help book, I was at a pivotal point in my life. I decided that my life purpose was to help people come together. I realized that many great leaders—Mother Teresa, Gandhi, Martin Luther King, John Lennon, for example—had united humankind. Maybe this seems obvious to you, but to me, it was a revelation. It was also my call to do the same.

I also became aware of how self-focused I had been my entire life. Whenever I had found myself in a position of power, I used it to benefit myself—never others. Then I wondered why the people around me were so selfish! Now and again, we all find ourselves in positions of relative advantage. Some jobs give us influence over certain people or policies. Some birth characteristics (unfortunately) come with social advantages. Some situations, such as discovering someone's insecurities or secrets, give us the upper hand in a relationship. But, at any moment, we can lose our privileges. Then, the way we treated other people will come right back to us. I vowed to keep this always in mind. To remember, at the top, what I needed when I was at the bottom. To remember how it feels to be judged before I judge. To extend the helping hand I yearned for when I was the one grasping. To be the light I needed in my times of darkness. To remember where I came from.

After years of suffering and selfishness, I wanted to do something meaningful. Becoming a self-help guru meant fulfilling that desire—and then some. Encouraged by various motivational speakers, life coaches, and spiritual teachers, I began to see my dark past as a resource. I didn't have to bury my suffering, my self-hatred, or my former addictions! I could share them. I could use them. I could help heal others.

I started a blog. Then, I started writing for bigger websites. Inspired by Brené Brown's TED talks about shame, I shared my imperfections, my self-doubts, my painful memories. I tore myself open and let the world see inside. After a lifetime of perfectionism and hiding, vulnerability was difficult. But once I connected with people who understood me, I couldn't get enough. I had spent most of my life feeling separate, misunderstood, and alone. While I was healing, I realized that I was *never* alone because I was an interconnected part of existence. Yet healing also changed my personality. I lost many of the friends I had. Taking a leadership role introduced me to my new tribe: people who understood me. The *real* me. These authentic connections gave me a high beyond that of any drug, any compliment, any achievement. I was hooked.

3

Writing my first book was an incredible catharsis. It also marked a turning point. My writing was no longer a mere hobby. Now, I had a product to sell. I had to put myself out there. This changed everything.

As soon as I had to sell myself, I realized how little there was to buy. I kept finding proof of how unqualified I was to help people. I wrote *The Love Mindset* when I was 24—much younger than the self-help gurus I admired. I didn't have a PhD. I didn't have a major publishing house backing me. I turned red when I talked to people, and I said "like" too much when I got excited. All my clothes were from the thrift store. I lived in a moldy basement. Who was *I* to help anyone?

Thus, my writings and teachings warped. Even though I still wrote about healing and self-love, I stopped sharing as vulnerably. I started talking about self-judgment as something I *had*. I thought that if I revealed how insecure I still was, I would only further delegitimize myself. Instead, I focused on giving people good advice and correct answers. That's what gurus do, after all.

The trouble with giving advice was that I had no idea what other people should do. So I just regurgitated the concepts I had learned from self-help. All the while, I watched those same concepts fail in my own life. I would tell people to stop caring about what others thought, yet my mood would crash from one critical comment. I would tell people to focus only on positive thoughts, but my mind was a minefield of anxiety and self-doubt. I would tell people to accept their bodies, yet I still sometimes felt ashamed of my skin (where my inner struggle externalized). Every time my practical experiences negated my teachings, I would fall into the deepest pit that a leader can fall into: the Fraud Hole. In that bleak mental underground, there is only darkness and a voice that chants, "Everyone hates me, and anyone who

4

doesn't will soon. Because I'm a fraud. I know nothing. I have nothing to offer."

Every time I dismounted the rollercoaster of inadequacy, I would get right back into selling the dream—not only to others but to myself as well. I wasn't scheming behind closed doors to manipulate and seduce people. Rather, I was weaving a story of how the world could and should be—a story I believed. Every time I arose from the ashes of shame, I would prod myself to hurry up and become a better leader. Every time I failed, I would tell myself I needed to try harder, practice more, do more. I needed to become who I pretended to be. The self-judgment I claimed to have healed once again spread like cancer. I got sick from my expectations. I suffocated my potential with my twisted ideas about what that potential should be.

Before I started my healing journey, I always thought that happiness was only a few pounds away. No matter how much weight I lost, it was never enough. No matter how much my stretch marks faded, they were never light enough. No matter how many blemishes healed, there was always one more. Every time I looked in the mirror, I'd say, "Maybe next time." Maybe next time, you'll be pretty. Maybe next time, you'll be perfect. Maybe next time, you'll finally be flawless. Not today, but maybe next time. It was the same after every coaching session, every Meetup, every video, every speech. I would pick apart everything I had said and done, and I would always find flaws. Once again, I was chasing the ever-elusive "next time."

And as I was busy ripping myself apart, I could help no one. I treated other people like I treated myself—like they were in need of fixing—while telling them that they weren't broken. I stunk of insincerity. Unconsciously, I drove people away. The meeting rooms emptied out. The messages and emails thinned. No one was buying what I was selling anymore, not even me.

It was a vulnerable time for me, not only emotionally but financially as well. A few months prior, I had quit the day job secured by my college education, which left me with five figures of student debt. Of the three life-coaching clients I had when I so optimistically handed in my four-week notice, two (rightfully) left. Of the few dozen people who had attended my weekly groups, only one remained (who was my friend before all this). The person who had been giving me public speaking opportunities not only stopped asking me to work with him but also refused to pay me for my last speech. I was confused and frustrated. I was broke and in debt. I felt like a fraud. I was breaking apart.

I would like to say that I had an epiphany right then and there, but I didn't. I think that, sometimes, we have to get lost before we can find ourselves. So that's what I did. I got helplessly lost. I began to wander within myself, searching for answers. Was something wrong with me? Was I not as peaceful and loving as I thought I was? Was I only pretending that I was all better? Did I know nothing about healing and happiness? Why couldn't I help people? Why couldn't *I* do what I was telling other people *they* could do? What if I wasn't who I said I was? What if I was just lying to myself to feel better about having wasted a decade on drugs and self-destruction?

I had no idea what to do. In desperation, I began to look outside myself. On my search, I found hundreds of answers from just as many experts. Each answer had a corresponding cookie-cutter solution. I hadn't designed an effective program. I didn't have a strong enough "personal brand." I wasn't using the correct modalities. I needed better copywriting. I needed a formula. On and on. Some of these tactics earned me money—at the cost of crippling guilt. The Fraud Hole grew deeper as I disconnected from everything I held dear. I tried everything. Or so I thought. I did what the experts said, and I did what my self-judgment said, but I forgot something. I forgot about that excited, red-faced girl in second-hand pants who just wanted to help people and feel understood.

In a moment of frustration, I broke down. I wanted to give up. I cried because I had no answers and no formula. I cried because I had no idea what I was doing, and I never would. I cried because I had lost my way, and I didn't think I would ever find it again. After my last tear fell, I expected to feel defeat, shame, helplessness. Instead, I found myself face to face with reality—the view I'd been avoiding all along. And reality was as it always had been: without meaning.

Reality was neither ugly nor ravishing. It was neither joyful nor depressing. It was neither good nor bad. It was neither endless suffering nor endless progress. It was not even something in-between. Reality was the raw data I hadn't analyzed, the full dictionary I hadn't turned to speech, the endless night sky before I chose a favourite star. They say, "You can be limitless," but this cannot mean limiting ourselves to only the positive, joyful, pleasant parts of life. True limitlessness includes everything, warts and all.

In reality, I wasn't a bad leader, but I was not a good one either. I wasn't a fraud or a liar, but I also was not a saviour or a martyr. I wasn't ruining people's lives, but I wasn't exactly helping them either. I hadn't cured all my insecurities and anxieties, but I also was not suffering as I once had. I wasn't perfect. I was a human being. I was doing my best. And, maybe, that was okay.

I crawled out of the Fraud Hole and surrounded it with caution tape. I apologized to my reflection. I reconnected with who I was when I first started my blog. Over the next year, I became more honest, more compassionate, and more intimate with the people I helped instead of trying to fix them. The more I did this for others, the more I reconnected with myself. I reached a deeper, more mature level of vulnerability than ever before. The more I practiced this approach, the more I realized how rare it was in the self-help world. I began to see the work I had so deeply loved in a harsh, new light.

My suffering, my clients' suffering, our culture's suffering—it was all connected. Previously disjointed memories came together in my mind. Standing on a scale for the fourth time in a day, obsessing over 0.2 of a pound. Advertisements with brand-new cars, brand-new couches, brand-new TV programs—everything you need to "be happy." Eating raw celery, hoping to shed enough pounds before a vacation. People talking about the next self-help book like they talk about the next yo-yo diet—like this would be the one to fix it all. Expensive seminars and packed workshops. How smoothly a 4-tips list leads to a 10-step program that segues into a 3-day breakthrough experience.

I realized that the self-help industry makes money more consistently than it makes people happy. There is a difference between helping people and helping people *buy*. There is a difference between showing people their potential and selling them on a dream. There is a difference between nourishing people's authentic desires and reinforcing their most tempting idealisms about the nature of reality. There is a difference between a guide and a guru.

Deeper than ever, I began to understand the suffering of the people I was trying to help. I saw how bombarded they were with advice from experts and sages. I recognized their perpetual confusion about which actions to take. I felt their self-blame and shame for not being able to do what other people claimed to have done. I empathized because I had been a victim of this suffering. Yet I had been a perpetrator of it as well. I had chased the carrot of Happily Ever After, and I had dangled that carrot in front of others. I had climbed into a golden throne marked "expert" while leaving those who followed me down on the ground. As a teacher, I had forgotten what I hungered for as a student. I began to see how fortunate it was that I hadn't succeeded.

I had failed at being a guru, but I didn't *want* to be a guru. I didn't want to pretend I had all the answers because I *didn't* have them. No one does. What a relief. Imagine how I felt: trying to find the perfect phrasing, the perfect tactic, the perfect method to change people's lives. What a load of responsibility! Of course I felt tormented. No one should (or needs to) bear such a burden. Imagine the size my ego must have been to think I had to—or even *could*—give people answers. Wouldn't this imply that, without me, they couldn't find their own? I wasn't only driving myself crazy; I was also playing narcissist. These were not my brightest moments, but I am not pure light. I am real, darkness and all.

Perhaps this story would be more romantic if I had been a *New York Times* bestselling author with many letters after my name when I had this epiphany. Perhaps it would be more dramatic if I had gained international fame and fortune in self-help before realizing that I wanted to play a different part in it. But that's not me, not my story. Alas, this is no great spectacle, no electrifying drama, no celebrity transformation story. This is real, messy, imperfect, and human— just like me.

This book is my gift to you, but the gift is not pure inspiration. This book is here to encourage and uplift you, yes, but it is also here to warn you. The warning I want to give is not about self-help but consumerism. There is a difference between a book that opens doors to *your* opportunities and a book that opens doors to the opportunities in someone's business.

A well-known marketing guru once said that smart businesspeople sell their customers on independence while breeding dependence. This model is what makes the multi-billion-dollar self-help industry churn. Tell people they can be free, but don't actually free them. After all, if you genuinely help somebody heal, you lose a customer. This kind of marketing is so widespread that it's become a source of comfort. Messages that break the mold seem alien and strange. Books that promise magic bullets for unattainable results sell like hotcakes, while books that encourage a slow, conscious approach to sustainable changes remain obscure. We buy into the promise of freedom, but not freedom itself. We buy into the idea of liberation, and we keep purchasing this idea in new packaging. We believe seductive notions about our potential, yet we are too afraid to explore it. As Marianne Williamson said, we fear our light more than our darkness.

Within you is a fountain of wisdom. And you sell yourself short every time you allow some authority to define your limitations and cage your potential. Even if that authority lives in your head. In your experience, you can find answers about who you are and what you want. A major obstacle to happiness is the belief that someone else needs to help you find it. All you need is a healthy dose of reality. And reality is a tightrope between fear and idealism—both illusions.

Consumerism relies on make-believe. We buy fad diets and get-rich-quick schemes because we mistake fantasy for truth. We suffer manipulation through blindness more than force. We don't understand ourselves, so we believe stories about who we are and what we need. All the while, our needs go unmet.

A hungry person is easier to seduce. What are you hungry for? What have you been craving for so long that you've settled for insufficient scraps disguising as real nourishment? What have you desired so much that you've allowed success stories and unrealistic claims to cloud your judgment? And whom have you trusted to feed your hunger for you? Have they done what is best for you, or have they done what is best for themselves? And whose job is it, at the end of the day, to look out for what is best for you?

It's not that we live in a selfish world. It would be too easy to become angry at the misleading advertising and authorities all around us. To pin the whole thing on some individual or corporation. To boycott them. Alas, we cannot blame one person, or even one company, for how things are. It is a systematic issue. It is a cultural issue. It is everyone's issue.

As a teenager, I became obsessed with "culture jamming." This means using a method of media to spread messages that undermine the authority of that media. This is not my main purpose here. I am not writing this book as a satire of self-help books, and I am not here only to criticize the way things are. I am not here to advocate for the complete overthrow of consumerism, and I am not here to condemn the economy or the self-help authorities. Rather, I want to make you more conscious of what you buy into—including the ideas that shape your experience. I am here to promote self-awareness, self-trust, and self-discovery.

Hope for the future lies in each of us looking within. By learning to feed your hunger, you can overcome the tempting illusions all around you. By discovering who you are, you can stop basing your self-image solely on other people's ideas about you. By connecting to your inner strength, you can stop cycling between idealistic illusions and self-hating disillusionment. By taking responsibility for yourself, you can stop relying on others to take responsibility for you.

Even with all the conflict in the world right now, I believe that the most tragic war of our time is the one within. A war between what we knew as children and what we've learned as adults. A war between wisdom and intelligence. A war between the natural colour of our hair and the colour we chemically impose upon it. A war between the manicured hedges and the untouched wilderness. A war between reality and fairy tales. A war between what we could learn about the world and what we are systematically taught. A war that can end in peace.

Like many external wars, your inner conflict has been a source of monetary gain for people you've never met. To find the peace you deserve, you must know yourself, understand yourself, trust yourself. Only by healing can you ensure that no one profits from your suffering.

I am aware of the irony here. I hope, by this time, you won't think I'm concealing it. I feel that this message is too important to allow its unsavoury form to erode it. Calling someone a two-faced hypocrite is not a compliment. Yet reality itself is hypocritical, many-faced, ironic. The quest for truth abounds with paradoxes.

I want you to know your truth because the lies have always hurt you, no matter how much you've tried to ignore the pain. I want to show you how much you already know and how capable you are of making great changes in your life and in the world. I want you to see that you've been the one helping yourself all along while someone else has been taking the credit. That, in the end, is what this book is all about. It is about you. It's about me. It's about all of us. It is a mirror.

I have tried my best to make this book into a reflection of the human experience. In case it is not always clear, please keep in mind that each time I say "you," I am also saying "I" and "we." I am on this journey with you. Anything I say about you applies to me as well. I have also tried to make this work more accessible by alternating pronouns between "he" and "she" whenever possible. However, older quotes herein favour "he" because that was once the norm, and I acknowledge that there are many people in the world whose gender does not fit neatly into one of two categories. Thus, I ask you to accept these pronouns—he and she—as attempted reflections of me, of you, of us. Language has perpetually interfered with my attempts to design a truthful mirror for the human condition. I hope that, in addition to my efforts to create such a work, you might try to consume it as such.

I invite you to journal with this book and discuss what you are learning with others who are curious about self-discovery. Explore. Experiment. This book has no value if it remains a set of intellectual ideas. If these words drive you to create music or art, create. If you need to cry, cry. If you need to laugh, laugh. Allow this journey to be whatever it must be, and never forget to take me with a grain of salt. Do not follow me. I am not your guru. Instead, follow the words you whisper to yourself in the hidden rooms of your con-sciousness—both afraid that they are true and hoping that they must be. You're not broken. You matter. You're stronger than you think.

Self-Awareness Meets the Inner Conversation

*The most fundamental harm we can do to
ourselves is to remain ignorant by not having the
courage and the respect to look at ourselves
honestly and gently.*

PEMA CHÖDRÖN

Whether or not you've been paying attention to it, you—like every other human being—move through each day leading on a ceaseless inner conversation. You talk to yourself about what is happening and what it means. You relate today's events to yesterday's struggles and tomorrow's possibilities. You define your character and decide which roles you'll play with others. You judge some parts of your experience as favourable and others as unacceptable. You decide what to fix and what to leave alone. You give meaning to each dream, each longing, each discomfort. You formulate ideas about what happens inside other people's heads.

Your inner conversation is more than the sum total of thoughts that roll around in your head from day to day. It is the relationship you have with yourself and how that relationship connects you to the rest of existence. It is the lens through which you perceive reality. Thus, it defines the world you think you live in—a place that might be radically different from the real world.

How you talk to yourself decides how you feel about yourself and others. It influences the choices you make about big and little things. It determines the actions you consider essential and the ones you consider dangerous, the desires you honour and the ones you repress, the plans you make for days to come and the lessons you learn from days gone. Your inner conversation decides the quality of each moment in your life; and beyond the quality of each moment, what else is there? What else matters?

Despite its value, many of us neglect our inner discourse. We seek the answers to our problems outside ourselves. We buy into the tempting idea that better life circumstances will bring us happiness. How could we not? After all, this message is plastered on our billboards, written into our movie scripts, and woven into our advertisements. Hypnotized by modern-day consumerism, we miss the obvious gaps in such logic. We all know people who seem to have everything but appreciate nothing. And for every imaginable misfortune, we can find examples of people who have blossomed from it. One person loses an arm and falls into alcoholism, shame, and despair. Another person loses an arm and becomes a world-renowned Paralympian. This difference is not inherent within the people or the situation. It is a consequence of how each person translates the meaning of losing an arm. How they respond to life's events comes down to what they tell themselves happened.

We seek fulfillment in money, accomplishment, approval, status. We seek it in other people. One particularly harmful idea carried by our cultural narrative is that you need to find someone who will love you. Imagine if we believed this about any other basic need: food, water, oxygen.

If you needed another person to provide you with those, you'd be considered dependent—if not disabled. Yet we so willingly put ourselves in this state with love.

If someone else notices our qualities and talents, we think those parts of us must be worthwhile. Our potential floats like an island in the sea—uncharted, unexplored. We long for someone to discover us, admire us, colonize us. But why must it be another person? Why can't *you* sail that voyage and explore yourself?

Perhaps you've already come across advice that urges you to "look within." For many of us, this message is encouraging, so we give it a shot. We try to build self-love by giving ourselves nice gifts, doing positive affirmations, and taking longer lunch breaks. We work on self-care by building better habits, setting goals, and nurturing our passions. It all seems nice, but somehow, it's not enough. This self-love thing seems weak compared to romance, and self-care is hard to sustain. In moments of frustration, we run to the fridge, the shopping mall, the website, the TV show—anything to fill the void. Why does it seem so difficult to do what is supposedly good for us? Sometimes, it seems we are wired for unhappiness, doomed to run around in circles chasing our tails.

The trouble with the way we look within is that we rarely go deeper than those who pursue money or status. We tend to believe that once we get the right attitude, the right habits, the right belief systems, everything will be perfect. We place happiness into the hands of some future event, and we use ourselves to reach it. We *think* we're looking within, but we're still dabbling near the surface: objectifying ourselves and then becoming frustrated when those objects do not bend to our will.

Our ideas about what lies within us keep us from open-minded self-exploration. Our unmasked selves do not look as we think they should, so we try our best to keep them out of sight. We hide from others, and we hide from ourselves. We neglect the gold mines of potential within us because we're too busy trying to make ourselves perfect. We overlook our deepest possibilities while we search for joy in shallow waters. But no amount of money, accomplishment, or romance will bring you joy until you learn to talk to yourself about joy (or until you stop talking yourself out of it).

To journey into your inner conversation, you must go deeper than you have ever gone before. Any of us can notice negative self-talk patterns or note the stories we make up about other people, but changing these patterns is possible only for those who see the *whole* picture. The inner conversation is like a forest. You might read a book about gathering tree sap or avoiding poisonous snakes, and that might be helpful. But when you get out there, the wilderness will not contort itself to match your knowledge about it. It will be as it is. Therefore, you must do the contorting.

Here, we meet self-awareness. When I use this term, I am referring to the practice of trying to observe yourself as you *are* and not just how you imagine yourself to be. If you do not call this self-awareness, that is all right. If this is not how you define self-awareness, that is all right too. You are entitled to your definitions. I am not here to change them. I am here to communicate something to you. You can embrace my definitions without surrendering yours. Words, after all, have no inherent meaning, but we will explore that deeper in future chapters.

Awareness is a process of seeking truth. The inner conversation is the place we're going to explore. A truth seeker needs both: to know *how* to look and *where* to look.

Without self-awareness, you can only go so deep into your inner conversation. You can only hear so much. You can only change so much. A person who doesn't understand

17

flowers might tug on them to make them grow. A person who doesn't speak the language of someplace might misread the locals' sentiments and intentions. Yet you are already such a flower, and your inner locals—your emotions, your body, your thoughts—are already speaking to you. If you don't learn the language of your experience, then how can you understand yourself? How can you help yourself?

And without exploring the inner conversation, your capacity for self-awareness can only take you so far. In fact, it can take you further from reality. To some degree, we all practice self-awareness—regardless of what we call it. We try to discover the truth about who we are. Like a bee needs pollen, we need to know ourselves. It is a gift to humans like spinning webs is a gift to spiders. However, unlike the spider's talent, ours contains the potential for its own abuse and neglect. Because we can give meanings to our impulses, we can neglect our most fundamental needs. Because we can form ideas about ourselves, we can judge and hate who we think we are. Because we can conceptualize ourselves as being separate from others, we can create lonely, distorted inner worlds. Because we can imagine what other people think of us, we can become paranoid or narcissistic. Thus, we must not only try to see ourselves more clearly but also ensure that we are looking at our actual selves and not crafting collages out of our assumptions.

At the crossroads between the questions that lead you inward and the answers you receive back from yourself, self-awareness meets the inner conversation. Each time you experience this encounter, you have the opportunity to make a choice. Will you allow yourself to look, to explore, to understand? Over time, these choices add up. Like quitting smoking, it gets easier with time. Self-neglect is an addictive habit too—one that you can break.

Each moment of self-honesty builds intimacy, trust, and compassion. The more you look, the more you'll love. Here, we face a paradox—our first of many. On the one hand, self-awareness cultivates self-love. On the other hand, you need at least a small dose of self-love to begin the journey of self-awareness. On the one hand, exploring your inner conversation will help you understand yourself. On the other hand, you need some degree of understanding to begin that exploration in the first place. At this first, essential contradiction, I meet you. Our journey together begins.

Everything you need for our adventure is already within you. Look. Look within—not with an agenda but with curiosity. Look with love. Think of how you do this to others. When you love people, you are curious about who they are, what they think, and how they feel. You watch them closely, wondering about their experience and what you can do to make it more enjoyable. You feel compassion for their pain and seek to make it more bearable. You are eager to learn the unique language of their existence. You want to understand them, inspire them, heal them. What if you could look at yourself this way?

The curiosity with which you ponder the people you love assumes that they're worth exploring. Do you assume the same about yourself? Do you know how many undiscovered riches there are in your experience? Throughout your life, you have embraced some things, and you have abandoned others. You have been assertive, and you have been calm. You have listened, and you have spoken. So you already know how to hold on, let go, speak up, shut up, light up, and calm down. You don't need anyone to tell you what to do. You can figure that out for yourself—if only you can unleash your wild curiosity about the mysteries within you.

Only *you* can allow yourself to explore the person in the mirror. Only *you* can coax yourself into a daring adventure to find your untapped potential. After all, who can see inside the deepest recesses of your imagination and manifest those wishes into your daily experience? Who can appreciate the subtle nuances of character you've acquired by overcoming your deepest fears? Who can acknowledge the demons that are no longer controlling you because of the work you've done to release them? Who can see the strength left behind in the wake of your toughest struggles? Who will see you for who you are—appreciating everything that is there, everything that is not, and everything that can be—if you do not? Who else *can*?

Your inner conversation is bursting with information. Learning to harness it will help you become an active participant in the creation of your life. You don't need to wait for someone else to notice your talents before nourishing them. You don't need others to accept you to feel accepted. You don't need to wait. You can begin, at any moment, to work on noticing, nourishing, and accepting yourself. You can work on being a better friend to your reflection. You can start listening to yourself like you wish other people would. You can become curious about who you are. You can begin to learn the language of your mind and body so you can decode it, understand it, speak it. You can work on understanding yourself instead of always trying to make yourself into someone else.

No matter where we go, having a best friend to laugh and cry with makes all the difference. Such a friend is irreplaceable. There will always be someone funnier, sexier, stronger, richer, but no one can take the place of our memories, our jokes, our secrets whispered in the night. You can develop this kind of intimacy with yourself. After all, you're already stuck with yourself for a lifetime. Why not improve this relationship?

Self-understanding is a lifetime endeavour. It is not a weekend seminar. It does not come in capsule form. Every moment is ripe with opportunities to understand yourself better. Yet the moment is empty-handed. *You* are the source. The potential for awareness exists in every moment because it exists, first and foremost, inside you. You are the one with an inner conversation waiting to be deciphered. You are full of ingredients waiting to be cooked into tantalizing flavours. You are waiting to be experimented with. A chemical reaction waiting to happen. A story waiting to be told.

No one can tell your story like you can. And when you do, it will be unique. You may practice awareness for years before you feel a moment of inner peace. Or you may struggle for decades, have an epiphany right as you have a gun to your head, and then spend another few decades trying to integrate that wisdom into your life. It's all right to be either one or neither one. Your journey will be different from the journeys of others. Allow it to be.

You can begin to introduce self-awareness to your inner conversation at any moment. Yet you cannot learn to do it from a book—especially not from this book. If you've ever studied a language, and then become lost in the reality of human conversation—confused by the lack of structure and rules—then you already know what I mean. If you have ever gasped in wonder at the beauty of someplace, and then become frustrated with the two-dimensional eyesore captured on your camera, you already understand. A book may guide a journey, but it will never *be* the journey. Reading about an adventure does not substitute going on one. You must drink this, eat this, put it in your blood so that, one day, you will reread these pages and see them as inadequate photographs of the newfound sacred space within you.

This book hopes to be like a shack on the outskirts of the jungle you are about to enter. Here you will find guides, tools, and anecdotes from a fellow explorer. I can help prepare you for your journey; there is no doubt about that. However, preparation is all that this book (or any book) can ever offer you. Visiting the guide shack cannot teach you what you must learn out there in the depths of your uncharted wilderness.

The purpose of this book, more so than to provide tricks and tips, is to encourage you to travel with your eyes open, your heart courageous, and your mind always ready to learn. The examples in these pages are like the flavours and tastes of a certain kind of cuisine. They are outcomes of a specific outlook, a certain understanding of how things go together. Examples cannot teach you what you will learn by exploring. Your inner path has been waiting inside you for much too long. It yearns for you. Our goal is to kindle that yearning. The fuel is already there. Let's set you on fire.

Let us walk together. We will talk about how to look and how to see, how to listen and how to hear, how to speak and how to make yourself heard. Our purpose is not to theorize and narcotize ourselves with arrogance—thinking we've evolved just because we've learned all the right things to say. Our task is more like learning to walk: putting one foot in front of the other and becoming efficient at it so that, one day, we can trek wherever we want.

Baba Dioum once said, "In the end, we will conserve only what we love; we will love only what we understand; and we will understand only what we are taught." This is what we are here to explore: understanding and, through understanding, love. Yet the teaching I embark upon here is not a lecture but an exploration, an adventure, an open-ended conversation.

After I release this book, I suspect I will feel that I haven't said everything I wanted to say and inadequately expressed the things I did say. My only antidote to such guilt is this: I am you talking to yourself. After you flip the last page, you will take over where I left off.

Part of my task is to leave you with some firewood and show you some pathways to find more. But my *ultimate* task is to encourage you to seek and find your own paths. I do not hope to show you the most sustainable way to gather kindling for the blaze inside your soul. More than anything, I want to show you the beauty of fire and awaken you to your inner urge—the same urge I found within me—to keep that fire burning.

Before You Speak

It is the province of knowledge to speak, and it is the privilege of wisdom to listen.

OLIVER WENDELL HOLMES SR.

To help with negative self-talk, many self-help gurus recommend positive affirmations. These, as you might be aware, are spoken statements meant to help you achieve a specific goal. There are affirmations for weight loss, self-love, and success. There are affirmations to help you battle cancer, become a better parent, and discover hidden spiritual powers. The theory is that repeating earnest statements to yourself will convince your mind that they are true. Sometimes this works. Most of the time, it doesn't. But why?

A person who undertakes the practice of saying affirmations to herself might be under the impression that she is starting afresh on a blank slate with a new goal. Nothing could be further from the truth. Though our affirmations-sayer might not be aware of them, there are already conversations about that goal within her. If you have ever interrupted a discussion to say something unrelated, then you know this: interruptions are often unwelcome. Especially when they are full of syrupy platitudes! An egotistical boss might enjoy an occasional bootlicking, but most of us are uncomfortable with false flattery. Especially when it comes from someone we know well. How strange would it be if you called your father one day and, mid-same-old-sentence, he began to butter you up—calling you a radiant, powerful money magnet who is worthy of joy and abundance? That would be at least absurd, if not alarming.

A major roadblock on the path to change is treating ourselves like blank slates. If you've ever suffered heartbreak, you know you cannot reclaim innocence. We cannot unexperience pain. We cannot unknow some unsavoury truth about the world. We cannot unlearn the lessons of the past. We can, of course, experience pleasures that put past pains into perspective. We can develop new attitudes that balance our self-protective ones. We can revise, amend, and update the lessons of the past, but we cannot delete them. Our life experience is an endless, cumulative conversation that may change in content and context but never in history. If you embrace a complete stranger, even in the downtown of a major city, you might get a positive reaction. But someone who's held a bitter grudge against you for a decade probably won't reciprocate your enthusiasm. Thus, cramming unfamiliar words down your own throat might feel inauthentic and unwelcome. Even if some so-called expert has endorsed these positive phrases, they might still feel like lies. And self-deceit does not lead to happiness. As the victim of the lie, you will feel betrayed. As the perpetrator, you will feel embarrassed. Your attempts at positivity might not only buckle but also backfire.

Can you march into a game of Double Dutch with your eyes closed, using nothing but willpower to help you jump in? Likely not. You don't need will, control, or micromanagement. You just need to look before you leap. This seems clear, yet we make such mistakes with ourselves. We try to change our behaviours by controlling them. We assume that self-control is a matter of augmenting our reactions, but our experience says otherwise. Trying not to feel or think a certain way is like trying not to think of a giant, green chicken when prompted. (Try it right now—I dare you!) The mind does not work this way. You cannot control the emotions, thoughts, or memories that torment you, but you *can* control how you choose to respond to them. And if you don't respond as planned, you can control your response to that failure. You can meet your disappointments with acceptance and curiosity instead of judgment and criticism. And when your reactions *are* favourable, you can notice and celebrate. You cannot directly control the conversation you are having with yourself, but you can control your *perception* of it and your *reaction* to it. You can influence your patterns by how you respond to them. You can accept everything and nourish what is best. And, after all, isn't that exactly what a best friend does?

When you first saw the title of this book, you might have thought it would be about positive self-talk. However, much like affirmations, most self-talk methods tend to focus on speaking while minimizing (or even ignoring) the importance of listening. Although speech may transmit loads of information, it does little to facilitate understanding. Before we can influence the inner conversation, we must first drift to the sidelines and watch it for a little while. Whether we're leaping into a game of Double Dutch or into the core of our emotional imbalances, jumping in too soon will only leave us tangled up and self-conscious. Thus, oddly enough, the art of talking to yourself begins not with speaking but with listening.

What does it mean to listen to yourself? Well-meaning advice instructs you to "follow your heart," "trust your inner voice," and "find your authentic self." But what do these things mean? We may seek what is "true" and "real," but in everyday life, our regrets and anxieties are just as real, and sometimes just as useful, as our dreams. Does the heart advise us to check if the stove is off before we leave the house? Even to the most confused truth seeker, this seems like a task for the head. But if the stove *was* on, and our checking prevented an accident, then maybe the head is not so bad after all. Even if we say that the heart consults us on meaningful choices, while the head deals only with menial day-to-day tasks, the confusion remains. If you find yourself at a critical decision point, such as leaving a relationship, you will find proof that you should stay and proof that you should go. Then, one day, you will look back and decide if your choice was correct. This decision is not likely to represent the ultimate truth of the situation. Rather, criticizing your past choices is a habit. So is justifying them. Depending on which habit you're in, you will either congratulate yourself for trusting your gut or scold yourself for lacking self-confidence. Every situation has ample proof for both interpretations. How are you to know which thoughts are trustworthy and which are not?

Many people search for the one magical, enlightened inner voice that will guide them toward everything they desire. Seeking the wise inner guru can be as problematic as seeking such gurus in the outside world. There is not a single person on this Earth who is always right. Not a single human being can answer all of life's questions. Not one man or woman can teach you a flawless philosophy that will fix all your problems. No one can do this. Why, then, should there be anything inside you—whether it is a heart, a voice, or an inner guru—that can?

In reality, there is a myriad of voices, answers, and words within you just like there is a myriad of stars in the sky. From the ancient to the modern world, various cultures have invented creative labels for the stellar constellations.

These labels often mirror the historical values and symbols of each culture. Growing up in the Ukraine, I learned about the "Big Bear" constellation. When I came to Canada, I learned to call it the "Big Dipper." In the Netherlands, they call those same stars the "Saucepan." In Germany, the "Cart." Like this, you can label your mental, emotional, and physical experiences. You can find a pattern of thought and feeling, isolate it from the rest of your thoughts and feelings, and call it "inner wisdom." You can find a cyclical pattern of behaviours, emotions, and thoughts, trace a box around that pattern, and call it a disorder. The labels you give to yourself, like the labels we give to star constellations, do not represent some universal truth about reality. There's no ethereal border around Ursa Major to block it off from the rest of the universe. And there's no such border around any part of your experience either.

Labelling star constellations helps us understand our relationship to them. It also helps us communicate about that relationship. So it goes for the inner conversation. Labelling our inner patterns helps us describe and share our experiences. But these labels are merely tools. They're only as accurate as they are useful. We label to help us understand reality better. Yet reality remains undivided.

Even if we observe some pattern about ourselves as an unshakable truth, it might disappear when viewed from a different perspective. When we label a star constellation, we observe its shape from Earth. We see a two-dimensional view of stars that exist in three-dimensional space. If we were to view these stars from another angle—from a nearby galaxy, for example—the patterns we see would shift. We would see something different. We would need new labels, new constellations, to make sense of our experience. To change perspective is to change perception. Labelling might help us communicate about minute parts of reality, but if we believe that those labels *are* reality, we trap ourselves in cycles of misunderstanding. As we try to sort our experiences into neatly labelled boxes, we find parts that fit into multiple categories and parts that don't fit into any. So we empty our boxes, think of some new labels, and start all over again. All the while, reality is as it is, unaffected by our misunderstanding.

In a moment of anxiety, for example, what could you say is the "problem"? Are your anxious thoughts the problem? Or is the feeling of anxiety the problem? Or is your body chemistry the problem? If you often worry, you might blame your thoughts. But where do these thoughts come from? And what about how you react to them? Then again, you might have a hormonal imbalance or too much caffeine in your system. Then, you could label your body chemistry as the problem. But what about your habits of creating (or allowing) that chemistry? And what about the parts of your self-image that affect those habits? We could go on and on like this. When we change our perspective, we change our perception. The organizational structure we've imposed upon reality begins to crumble, and we find ourselves, once again, facing the incomprehensible night sky.

Most of us are trying to avoid this overwhelming feeling of starting again. Thus, we look for experts to tell us what is right and wrong. On the journey of self-awareness, however, you will not find right or wrong. You will not find one magical inner voice to advise you on all your plans, and you will not find one evil inner voice to blame for all your troubles.

When we listen to ourselves with callous objectivity—trying to diagnose and eradicate our problems with effective solutions—this "listening" rarely works. Think of the people who treat you this way: those who can't see beyond their labels and judgments of you. Those who only "listen" for long enough to decide which advice to give you. It feels horrible. This same attitude prevents us from hearing our inner conversations. When we feel like someone has an agenda, we resist. Trying to fix ourselves while pretending to love ourselves doesn't work. We don't heal through objectification. We heal through understanding. We need to feel appreciated by the people who help us—ourselves included.

To hear your inner conversation, you must learn to listen differently. It is my hope that, throughout these pages, I can show you what this kind of listening might involve and how it can transform the way you talk to yourself. But don't forget that, at the end of the day, I am only a human being lying next to you on the soft summer moss, pointing up at the undivided night sky. Just because I am beside you, my perspective is a little bit different. Thus, so is my perception. I may point, but you must see. I may help you listen, but you are the one who must hear.

Searching for the "Right" Answers

Believe those who are seeking the truth. Doubt those who find it.

ANDRÉ GIDE

✳ ✳ ✳ ✳ ✳ ✳ ✳ ✳

I once believed that the famous phrase "know thyself" alluded to the ideas in this book: understand yourself, discover yourself, love yourself. Throughout history, however, these words have carried another meaning—one that is not only different but arguably opposite. For example, this phrase was carved into the Temple of Apollo where ancient Greeks went to consult with the Delphic Oracle. Far from encouraging visitors to discover their unique path, "know thyself" warned them not to forget their mere mortality and not to dare miss consulting the gods about their choices. "Know thyself" meant "know your place." Yet even in Greek times, these same words carried another meaning. In the writings of wise philosophers, the phrase was a reminder to "know your own truth," specifically apart from the truth given to you by others. The disparity between these two meanings is as relevant today as it was in the 10th century. It echoes a

31

familiar conflict: a clash between the answers we learn and the ones we already have.

To begin listening to your inner conversation, we must start here, instead of starting elsewhere, for a reason. To explore yourself as you are, you must break free of your preconceived notions about this "self." To find the answers to your questions, you must break free of your assumptions. You cannot write in a notebook that is already full. You cannot hear the subtle melody of one harp over a thundering orchestra. You cannot fall in love with your face if you do not take off the mask you've painted with society's expectations.

So many questions bloom in the human mind. There is so much we wonder about, so much we do not know. Who am I? What is the purpose of life? What is possible? What should I do with myself? How should I live? To all your questions, you have received answers. It might appear that you found these answers on your own, unguided by the outside world, but this is an illusion. We are all students of the environment. Some of us learn consciously: picking through what others say and matching it to our experience. However, most of us learn automatically: taking other people's opinions as ultimate truths. Like this, oracles claiming to be in touch with all-knowing gods have shaped your inner conversation. And they have reminded you to know yourself—to know your place.

Throughout human history, there has never been a shortage of authorities giving us the "right" answers. Answers about how to build our homes, gather our food, and help our society. Answers about our origins, our purpose, and the meaning of our lives. Answers about how to relate to one another and how to raise our children. How to lose weight, be happy, and make more money. How to heal various illnesses of mind and body. How we should feel, think, and act. Answers about who we are and what we need.

You have already received thousands, if not millions, of answers over your lifetime. Some, you have discarded. Some, you have disregarded. And some, you have internalized and accepted. You've allowed them to become voices in your head—ones that advise your decisions and inform your personality. This process has not been a completely conscious one, but perhaps it hasn't always been *uncon*scious. Maybe there have been times in your life when you've resisted an authority figure's advice because you thought you knew better. Maybe you've experienced this so rarely that you can't remember its ever happening. Or maybe you've experienced this so often that you rebel against every authority that comes your way. I have played both roles. I have been a "good girl," and I have been a paranoid, conspiracy-theory-toting activist. Neither brought me any closer to the truth.

When we find ourselves in a difficult situation of any sort, there are often two "easy" choices: passive submission and violent resistance. They are easy because they are automatic, reflexive. This situation is no exception. When we realize how little control we have over our lives and how much outside forces work to manipulate us, we tend to either shut down or take up arms. Neither response gets us far. Aggressive rebellion wears down our inner peace and prevents us from seeking peaceful solutions. This traps us in cycles of unhappiness where we trust no one and perceive flaws in everything. And blind obedience robs us of the choices we *can* make and prevents us from controlling the things we *can* control. This makes us feel like we are missing out on life and wasting time. Neither of these shortcuts can lead us to the truth. Awareness, on the other hand, can.

The Addiction to Quick Fixes and the Static Self

As a preteen, I did hundreds of tests with alluring titles like "What is your personality?" and "Which animal best describes who you are?" I was searching for a label: a static definition of my identity. I wanted to figure out who I was the same way I could find the answer to 12 plus 6. I wanted something final, decisive, ultimate. Thus, I avoided opportunities for growth, change, and self-discovery. I could not progress because I didn't know I was a work *in* progress.

Curiously, when I did these quizzes, I was dishonest. When asked if I was more likely to go to a party or stay at home, I would click "party" though I could count the number of party invitations I had ever received on one hand. I wasn't just a static thing. I was some *other* static thing. I would lie to myself because I believed my experience was wrong. I was a complicated math equation to which I'd peeked the answer in the back of the book, and I worked as hard as I could to make that answer correct. I wasn't aware of my inner conversation because I didn't *want* to know myself. I wanted to be like the girls in the movies. I wanted a mask.

I thought I was fat, blemished, and unattractive. I had too many stretch marks and not enough sex appeal. To fix these issues, I wanted the solution to be final, decisive, and ultimate as well. I wanted the one diet, one trick, one pill that would fix me. When a miracle remedy or magic potion failed, I'd throw it into my mental bucket of wrong answers. Then, I'd resume my search for the perfect quick fix. I was looking for salvation, but salvation would not come, could not come. I was trying to become someone, but I already *was* someone. How can any living thing become anything except what it is? Like this, I suffered. I hid from myself.

Masks are addictive. On every bus stop billboard and during every commercial break, we see images of who we should be. These, in turn, lead us to ask the wallet-emptying question: "How can I become what I should be?" We try. We buy. But every time we think we've reached perfection, it eludes us again. Every time we think we've crafted the perfect mask, it cracks. We see a so-called flaw. We see a so-called flawless person. We panic. We buy, buy, buy. We spend all our earnings and energy on trying to fix ourselves—trying to get our fix of worthiness.

Thus, we become addicted to so-called right answers. We try to impose static ideas upon our chaotic, dynamic experience. We crave quick fixes, magic bullets, and miracle solutions because we fear who we think we are. We're convinced that our true selves are so ugly, so wrong, so unacceptable, so broken that we work as hard as we can to conceal them from view. Like this, we suffocate our potential. Like this, we become perfect targets for shame-and-guilt-inducing advertisements.

For an almost insignificant amount of time objectively, but much too long ethically, I tried this kind of marketing. I had learned the "hurt 'em and heal 'em" approach from various gurus. This philosophy claims that you can't help people if you don't show them *how* you can help them. You can't heal a wound that's unacknowledged or hidden. The only way to show people what you can do, the gurus say, is to aggravate their wounds and then demonstrate your expertise in healing them.

This approach is not intrinsically evil. It can be helpful when used by people who can heal the wounds they're agitating. A massage therapist may need to hurt you to remove a knot. A surgeon may need to cut you open to remove a tumor. A sports coach may need to put his team through rigorous training. A life coach or therapist may need to ask a tough question or suggest a painful exercise.

But even this sort of healing has its limitations. The massage therapist can work out your knots, but he cannot fix your daily stressors or your patterns of poor posture. The surgeon can remove a tumor, but she cannot remove its mysterious causes or prevent future tumors. The coach can increase his players' skills, but he cannot instill within them a sense of responsibility for becoming the best they can be. Neither the life coach nor the therapist can ensure that a client's epiphanies will turn into sustainable habits.

There are plenty of experts who realize these limitations: people who teach methods of self-healing. This is progress, but even these authorities have a tendency to establish dependence. They encourage us to heal our wounds, but they specify a treatment procedure. They create the impression that our answers must come from external sources. Rare are those who encourage people to look within for their own understanding and learn to manage their own healing. They are rare because such messages of deep self-trust can only come from people who practice it. They are also rare because it is difficult to teach *only* self-trust—a predicament I face in writing this book. After all, if I trusted your healing potential, wouldn't I just leave you alone with it? Wouldn't the most trust-filled teaching be no teaching at all? This is another blatant hypocrisy—one I undertake consciously. As I see it, if we were to mute all the teachings on self-trust, we would not hear silence. All around us is an uninterrupted monologue that breeds self-doubt. Thus, to speak the opposite is a kind of balancing act.

We cannot remove the possibility of mistrust. And we cannot remove the possibility that this mistrust will make us crave quick fixes, static self-concepts, and "right" answers. These possibilities might always exist. Any piece of advice comes with some risk of creating dependence. What we *can* do is add trust to the mix so it can neutralize the addictive impulses. The invention of the car did not necessitate shooting all the horses and burning down all the carriages. To learn your truth, you need not destroy each shred of advice that tells you to know your place.

Once you trust yourself, you will look within. There, you will learn why neither the static mask nor the quick fix can lead you to the truth. The mask is solid, and you are ever-changing. The quick fix is a final answer, and you are an endless conversation.

Trusting Yourself

A few years ago, my travels led me into the coastal jungle of Costa Rica. At first, I was confused. Where were all the birds? Where were the animals? My disappointment did not last. As I looked closer at each tree, each branch, each patch of ground, I found what I was seeking. Trails of leaf-cutter ants creeping along gnarled vines. Howler monkeys sleeping with their tails curled around taupe branches. A baby sloth reaching for a leaf to snack on. I realized that my expectations of the jungle came from watching videos that would zoom in on each point of interest. I was dependent on external guidance. Alone, I had to use my *internal* camera to observe the world around me. I had to accept responsibility for controlling my focus.

To introduce self-awareness into your inner conversation, you must take responsibility for that introduction and, ultimately, take responsibility for yourself. Perhaps this makes you uncomfortable. But why? "Laziness," you might say. But what does it mean to be "lazy"? You are not too lazy to sleep when you feel tired. Why would you be too lazy to do something just as self-nourishing and important? Too often, our hesitation to explore ourselves comes from a lack of self-trust. More accurately, broken self-trust. Maybe you have taken responsibility in the past and failed. Maybe the philosophies and dogmas that you learned at a young age labelled you as untrustworthy. Maybe you have found (or find) yourself in relationships and workplaces that repress your authentic desires. Maybe your culture condemns the passions you have long held within you. You have learned myths and legends about the dangers of your inner jungle. Thus, you have always waited for the next guided tour to start, never daring to explore on your own.

We have learned to mistrust ourselves. A child does not mistrust her instincts. Imagine how tiresome (and maybe even impossible) it would be for an infant to learn to walk with chronic self-doubting thoughts. Should I really keep trying? I am failing a lot. Everyone is watching. Maybe I don't want it badly enough. Why can't I get it right? I've been stuck on this crawling thing for much too long now. Maybe this means I'm not supposed to walk. Maybe I'm not the kind of person who walks. Maybe I'm just a "crawler."

We have learned to mistrust our desires, our instincts, our gentle compulsions. Be sure that the child's desire to walk is no stronger than your desire to do what is natural to you. The child simply has not learned any other mental skills but to follow what is pulling her from within. She has nothing to distract her and nothing to shame her. She is free to trust because trust is the only option. Imagine that sort of freedom. Or should I say "remember"?

As we grow up, we learn to be afraid of our desires. Thus, we learn to micromanage them. We lose touch with our own answers because they receive too much negative feedback. The child feels that some things are right, but other people tell her they are wrong. Then, other people tell her what is right, but it feels wrong to her. Her inner guidance becomes so incompatible with her culture and conditioning that she begins to question herself. Am I wrong or is society wrong? All proof seems to point to the former. She locks away her wisdom along with her self-respect and then wonders, with every coming year, why everything feels so hollow.

Of course, some people choose the other option: to label society as wrong. Yet this might not bring them any closer to the truth either. Fighting the institutions who teach us to mistrust ourselves is one thing. Developing self-trust is another. While you are welcome to undertake any activism you choose, our purpose here together is not to subvert our culture or incriminate our conditioning. Rather, we can simply notice that society's teachings place numerous obstacles on the path of self-awareness. We can notice them, and then go around them.

Few institutions would dare to encourage self-trust. Instead, most authorities teach us to become placid participants in various systems. They do not teach us to be happy. If anything, they underline the dangers of freedom and the importance of control. Because these notions are so common—in our schools and churches, at the dinner table, and on the evening news—we begin to learn what we think is a universal truth: we must hold ourselves together. We learn that if we let ourselves go, we will become evil, lazy, savage. We learn the importance of pressure and restraint. We learn to repress our genuine desires because they're incompatible with society's expectations. We learn that if we are not doing well in a school subject or a self-improvement plan, then we are not pushing ourselves hard enough. We learn that people who succeed are examples of this kind of pushing. We learn that those who stop doing something only because it feels wrong are lazy. Even people who oppose one institution's dogma often end up buying into another's. It is difficult to escape these teachings because they are so ubiquitous.

Until we address our lack of self-trust, no method of self-help will work. No method of self-help *can* work. You can begin by realizing that mistrust is an acquired habit. Remember how you learned to doubt your nature. Remember how many times you've heard that if you do not take action to correct and control yourself, you will cause harm. How many examples have you seen of people who give in to their impulses and commit heinous crimes? Clearly, these people trusted their instincts—and look what happened. You've learned time and time again that human beings are not trustworthy.

There is a persuasion tactic used by salespeople called "the double bind." It helps a seller get what he wants from you by presenting you with two choices that both benefit him. An example is "Do you want to buy this now or later?" Both choices assume that you're going to buy. By narrowing your options, the salesperson dictates your outcomes. Most people fall into the trap, kicking themselves later as they become aware of all the *other* options (such as not buying at all). Thus, the double bind often leads to buyer's remorse. Like this, we buy useless contraptions as well as inauthentic ideas about who we should be. In the end, such acquisitions can only lead to regret.

You have learned that your only two options in life are to surrender to your flawed nature or control yourself by following some code of conduct. Every institution and expert has a set of ideas about why your nature is so awful and a set of principles to fix it. Some emphasize your laziness and give you rules to enforce self-discipline. Others emphasize your propensity for suffering and provide you with steps to inner peace. Following a numbered path will teach you to trust *something*, and this will certainly feel better than trusting nothing at all, yet you will find yourself in an invisible double bind. You will continue to assume that your natural state needs repair.

When we take a closer look at this idea of the flawed human nature, it doesn't seem to hold up. How can you naturally be lazy if you feel driven to do some things and avoid others? Surely, we cannot be lazy with everything, no matter how little willpower we have. We all have unique motivations that propel our behaviours. Just because our motives do not fit with those of our school or church does not mean they are invalid.

How can your natural state be gluttony if you experience correlated side effects every time you overdo it? Surely, those side effects are just as much a part of your nature as the desires that result in them.

How can the natural state of your mind be to create suffering if that same mind can help create peace? Most children do not seem to suffer, and they have minds. Even if we ignore this and propose that suffering begins to develop at a specific age—that the adult mind is bound to suffering—we still miss the mark. How can we label the nature of anything by one of its stages or parts? You wouldn't claim that hunger is your natural state even though you are often hungry.

So it goes with morals about sin. Some say our nature is sinful, and we must learn to be good. Yet this is like saying that the nature of our garden is to grow weeds, and we must learn to plant flowers. The garden can do *both* because there is the potential for both. It is the same with the human being.

Look within you—is there not a conscience? Is there not a desire to feel loved and love other people? Is there not a drive to preserve beautiful things? Is there not a sense of responsibility for doing something meaningful with your life? Is there not a wish to influence the world in a positive way? Is there not a yearning to heal the wounds of your past and cultivate peace of mind? These are all facets of the human experience. They are as much a part of your nature as your suffering is.

Some hypothesize that certain people are born without a conscience. They say these people are destined to follow only the path of darkness. Even if this were true, then such a person would be an exception rather than a rule. We do not base our diagrams of the visible colour spectrum on what colour-blind people see. Why would we base our understanding of human nature on what we assume is happening in the minds of a small subset of the population? This is not only illogical but also dangerous and manipulative. When we allow the concepts that we systematically accept as true to define our limitations, those limitations become real. If we believe that we are broken and need some doctrine or expert to fix us, we will feel weak. We will then treat ourselves as weak. How, then, could we ever discover our strength? The cycle is self-perpetuating.

If someone dances with her urge for violence and ignores her conscience—however faint that conscience might be—how can we say she trusts herself? Surely, her self-trust is selective at best. Human nature, even if it includes violence, also includes the desire to love and connect with other people. Our nature might include deviant passions, but it also includes the ability to direct those passions into activities that are not only harmless but also productive. How can the murderer be an example of self-trust if he ignores so many aspects of that self in the name of one compulsion?

"Humans," Michael Shermer once said, "are pattern-seeking, story-telling animals." From the world around you,

you have learned which patterns to seek and which stories to tell. Your unconscious inner conversation has helped you mimic the people around you rather than understand yourself better. When you learn, from a young age, to fear, ignore, and suppress parts of your experience, you can only tell half the story. Thus, you remain an acquaintance to your reflection instead of an intimate friend. To live how you *feel* is right takes the same effort as to live how you're *told* is right. The work is the same. What is different is the reward. No amount of approval and no size of achievement can ever fill the space reserved for your opinion of yourself.

Of course, in the real world, we need both. We cannot live *only* by our own expectations. I wouldn't suggest that you drive on the opposite side of the road simply because you "feel that it's right." Self-trust is not about rebellion, and it's not about hedonism. It's about realizing that all your experiences—your thoughts, your emotions, your dreams—are valid. They exist for a reason. Accepting this reality does not require you to believe each thought, act on each emotion, or fulfill each dream. Quite the contrary, embracing each part of your experience gives you the ability to understand it, explore it, and integrate it. Instead of labelling your emotions as problems to solve, you can see them as signals to interpret. Instead of judging your desires as shameful aberrations, you can learn to meet them in healthier ways. Instead of calling yourself critical names when you cannot build or break certain habits, you can explore your motivations. You can become a student of yourself rather than always seeking a wiser teacher.

Once you begin to trust yourself, you will understand why nothing else has worked. If you have spent years trying to make changes that don't stick, cried countless tears trying to save relationships that fail, and used up all your patience on trying to feel something more than a ceaseless return to desperate emptiness, realize, first and foremost, that you are *not* flawed. You have never been flawed. You have never been broken. Rather, you have misunderstood yourself. You have failed at fixing yourself because you don't need to be fixed. You have been searching for answers, but you *are* the answer. You have been looking for the path, but you *are* the path. You have been working on the perfect mask, but you already have such a beautiful face. You have been trying to become something, but you already *are* something.

No tree tries to become a certain kind of tree. No flower tries to become a certain kind of flower. The tree and the flower open up to the sun and soak up water. Thus, they grow into themselves. No judgment. No expectations. No commentary. Your task is the same. If you can stop trying so hard to become who you think you should be, and instead commit to understanding and nourishing yourself, you will bloom into whatever kind of person you are. Taking responsibility for yourself is about self-care, not self-repair. Once you learn to feed yourself, you will better understand your hunger.

Maybe you neglect yourself because you don't know who you are or what you need. Yet this is like saying you're not flexible enough to take a yoga class. You become flexible *by* stretching, and you discover yourself *by* exploring. Surrender to the process. Let yourself learn. You don't need to have all the answers. On the contrary, your task is to observe and be humble. When I opened my eyes and my mind to the jungle around me, I surrendered to it. I let it teach me. And you can let your inner jungle teach you.

With closed minds tangled in double binds, we often forget about the big picture. We forget that we are participants in a larger pattern. We try to control our moods, and we try to control other people's opinions of us. Then, we lose self-confidence when we fail. We misunderstand what we *can* control. Thus, we waste our lives controlling what we cannot. We forget that if we stop micromanaging the universe, it doesn't stop existing. Life goes on. Things are already a certain way. The key to trust is humility. You did not invent the human condition. You did not design the human being. Swapping judgment for curiosity is not only an act of self-respect but also an act of surrender.

Allow yourself to trust that the bigger pattern of life resides within you as much as you reside within it. Trust that there is already something going on. Trust that, when you are not holding yourself together so tightly, you will not fall apart. Trust that the flow of life contains you, is bigger than you, and will take care of you—if you let it. Let yourself experience this. Let yourself practice. You cannot build self-trust by reciting affirmations all day. You have to get out there and take some chances. Experience life. Experience yourself. Taste yourself fully. It won't just give you happiness and meaning; it'll also protect you from the flavour experts who are out to sell you on being a better recipe than you already are.

The World's Foremost Expert on Yourself

Many of us buy into the dream of a painless summit of eternal bliss. We believe that once we reach this goal, we will be happy, healthy, and beautiful forevermore. Our desperation to find this place makes us buy magical maps that promise to show us the way. Full of optimism, we begin to walk the path, convinced that we are ascending, awakening, evolving, transforming into a higher species of human. After much climbing, we eagerly search for our promised perfection.

Instead, we find the same old worries, impulses, and obsessions. Confused, we consult our map, but it looks nothing like the terrain around us. We trace our fingers along the path, trying to find where we went wrong. We flip the map upside down. We bring it closer, then further away. There is no use. We are lost. In frustration, we begin to blame ourselves. "How could I get lost? I should have studied the map more closely! Rita said this map was great. Why did I get lost, and she didn't? This always happens to me!"

Just as we sit down in exhaustion, a mapmaker pops out of nowhere. She seems to understand exactly how we feel. She asks us if we are experiencing disappointment, self-blame, shame. She empathizes. She comforts us. She tells us it's not our fault. She says our map is wrong. Blaming the map, rather than blaming ourselves, restores our self-respect (at least for the moment). Then, the mapmaker sells us on another map—a better, more accurate one. Our optimism returns. To the magical, painless summit we go!

Then, despite our best efforts, we get lost again. And again. And each time we become frustrated, another mapmaker shows up to criticize the guide in our hands and sell us a "better" one. Blaming the map upholds our self-confidence for some time, but after a while, we face a familiar choice: submit or resist. We give up the climb, stew in self-judgment, and wrap our dreams in resentment. Or we lash out—perhaps at ourselves, or perhaps at those mapmakers. Regardless of whom we blame, we are still stuck in the same cycle. We cannot find the truth if we're too busy searching for someone onto whom to peg the lies.

Blame is a cigarette. It soothes your mind and your muscles when you take a drag on it. It feels like it helps. If you do this for long enough, often enough, you forget that it helps only because it takes away the same stress it creates. Blame is an addiction. Yet, like any addiction, blame is a symptom of something larger—a lack of awareness. When you watch a fly beating itself against a closed window, can you blame either the fly or the glass? Of course not. Thus, awareness eradicates blame.

If you've been stuck in a cycle of idealism and disillusionment, forgive yourself. It's not your fault. But it's not those mapmakers' fault either. They are stuck too. When you cannot stick to a diet program, there will always be someone to sell you a supposedly better one. And how can you blame that person? Why would a diet salesperson teach you that diets don't work? All those mapmakers, they subsist on that mountain. They live in the illusion too.

The missing ingredient, all along, has been trust. Each time you become hopeful that another product, another fix, another miracle solution will make it all better, you strengthen your self-doubt. And each time you become disillusioned with your purchases, you strengthen it further. And what does this mistrust do except make you more likely to buy another product, another miracle solution?

Maybe you've already suspected this. Perhaps, from time to time, you have wondered if there really *is* a magical peak at the end of the road. This train of thought leads to liberation, but on that same track also runs a freight train full of regret for wasted time and energy. To transcend blame and mistrust, you must face the inevitable: you've been barking up the wrong tree. This realization might be painful, but avoiding it will hurt you much more in the long run.

No map can lead you to a place that doesn't exist. No miracle diet can help you achieve a sculpted body that does not need nutrition or exercise. No self-help seminar can help you become a perfect person who never says the wrong thing. No guidebook can gain you the approval of every single person you come across. These outcomes are not real.

47

They are illusions. Self-improvement requires self-understanding, and self-understanding is not a place but a path. And there are no maps for *your* path because it doesn't exist yet. You must create it yourself by conquering the unexplored territory within. Only Arthur could draw the sword Excalibur from the stone, and only *you* can map your path of self-discovery.

You might still long for someone to show you the way. You may look for, as one of my clients liked to say, "an adultier adult" than you. Someone who isn't as lost as you think you are. Someone wiser, smarter, braver. We peek over the shoulder of our neighbour to copy the answers— the correct answers to life.

In school, I loved getting the right answers. I especially excelled in subjects like math that had firm, final answers. I didn't do so well with art or music. In the privacy of my bedroom, I had no shortage of creativity, but I had no idea how to use it at school. My goal was not to learn but to get good grades and thus avoid punishment. I would review my teachers' expectations for every assignment and make a plan to meet them. In personal essays, I wouldn't express how I felt as much as how I thought the teacher wanted me to feel. I remember writing, "As an immigrant, I feel so privileged to be allowed to access the amazing education system in this country." Yet I knew, full well, that what I had learned in the Ukraine in grade one didn't appear in the Canadian curriculum until grade five. I'd give the "right" answer, but it wasn't always true. In art, I could do neither. I didn't understand the expectations. I would provide what the teachers asked for, but that was never enough. In art, you had to be creative, make it your own, have original ideas. But how could my imagination be free when I needed to earn a high grade for my creations? I lived under the assumption that everything had a correct answer. I couldn't function in social environments with inaccessible or unclear answers. When I left school, nothing was like math. Life was like art, and I was bad at it.

The belief that there is one correct answer to every problem is a mental impediment. This kind of thinking is incompatible with self-awareness. To believe in ultimate right answers is to build a wall around one small corner of a large apartment, live there, and then complain that there's not enough space. Life encompasses all answers, including those that appear to be opposites. The inspirational quotes we love to share with one another reflect this paradoxical tendency. They say insanity is doing the same thing over and over again while expecting different results. Then, they say being able to do the same thing over and over again in the *absence* of results is called perseverance. They tell you to go with the flow. Then, they remind you that only dead fish go with the flow. They say to cut toxic people out of your life without looking back. Then, they say to give kindness to those who are unkind because they need it most. Fixating on one of these answers without leaving room for its opposite is like trying to run on one foot—it's possible, but to those who have two working legs, it's simply inefficient.

Trying to implement one specific tactic or piece of advice exclusively is a demoralizing process. No matter how useful it is right now, every piece of advice will no doubt become useless in a few years, few months, or even a few moments. Each piece of advice is only as helpful as the situations that require it, and no further. Even today, when looking at the clichés above, you resonated with some more than others. If you were to reread that paragraph in three years, or even three weeks, you might resonate with something different. Besides your name, your state of being alive, and your existence within the oneness of the universe, few things will remain constant throughout your lifetime. The right answers tend to change like the wind.

Imagine that some sailors come to you before a journey to get advice about the wind's direction. You tell them it's blowing north. But by the time they set off, it starts blowing west. Imagine those sailors blaming themselves for sailing poorly without ever questioning your advice. It sounds ludicrous, yet this kind of thing happens all the time.

If you put yourself in the expert's shoes, you might feel guilt or shame about misleading others in such a way. But what about misleading yourself? What about allowing others to mislead you? Do you wait for the great Wind Expert to tell you which way the wind blows?

Throughout time, many people have claimed special knowledge about how our minds work, how we behave, why we are here, what we're meant to do, how to be happy, and so on. Some of these experts gained authority through marketing, while others gained it through education. Educated experts can appear to be the most "adulty" adults of them all. Learning from them may inspire you and inform you, but at the end of the day, they draw their conclusions from the same resource you have: awareness of human experience. Of course, there is a difference between a controlled study that measures the behaviours of 200 people in a laboratory and you studying your own behaviours on a Tuesday afternoon. Yet both reveal some part of the truth. It is in the act of examination, observation, and questioning that we become more acquainted with something or someone. The scientist sorts through data to make conclusions, and you can do the same. After all, you already have more information about yourself than any other person alive. You are the world's foremost expert on yourself.

Other people can inspire you. They can guide you. But in the end, you have the power to understand yourself—and even understand the human condition—as much as (if not more than) any well-studied academic. Your understanding can encompass objective observation *and* empathy. You can formulate ideas about yourself *and* compare those ideas to your direct experience. Most people will either use logic to analyze you or empathy to relate to you. It is a rare breed of person who can do both. Yet for each of us, such a person lives in the mirror. You can observe your patterns of past and present, *and* you can discover the beliefs and desires that sustain them. You can accept yourself as you are *and* work on making life-altering changes. You can study what is *and* imagine what can be.

We had better leave some things to the experts (like welding and surgeries). But must we compartmentalize the answers to human suffering into specialized professions, and then label those people as authorities while always thinking of ourselves as their subordinates? Not only do such practices impede self-discovery and self-understanding, but they also do a great disservice to those well-studied experts. When we treat people like saviours, we neglect to take responsibility for ourselves. Thus, those who try to help us always come up short.

Asking people for help or advice is valuable and often important. It can give you a new perspective. Someone who has had experience with what you have suffered can guide you. As an old Chinese proverb teaches, "To know the road ahead, ask those who are coming back." Even someone who reads about your suffering in a book could teach you a useful tactic or help change your outlook. Consulting others about your problems is not inherently harmful. It can be valuable and even life-changing. The harm lies not in seeking help but in allowing other people to define your potential and your limitations. We all came out of the womb naked—experts included. Some people gain authority by marketing. Others by education. Some by experience. Others by inheritance. You do not need to bow down in front of any other human being.

Sometimes, it isn't the experts who label you as inferior; it's your thoughts. The person helping you might urge you to trust yourself, yet you might still believe that this person knows better than you do. Thus, when he gives you an example, you might take it as an instruction. That might happen to you with this book! The key is not to shun external help but to develop a relationship with your inner feedback. Thus, you can take what you need and disregard the rest.

Perhaps you idolize expert opinions because you don't think you are smart enough to figure it out on your own. But what is "smart"? Is intelligence a static state? Consider this example from my life. When I was a kid, my parents told me I was smart and good at math (presumably, because they were). They forced me to study math textbooks a few grade levels ahead. I studied every night. I made many mistakes, but after hundreds of attempts, I learned. Then, in class, I excelled while other children made those same mistakes I had made. Except they made theirs in class, and there was no time to try a hundred times in class. My parents also said I was not musical or athletic. In those areas, I was the slowest in my grade. I thought this was a matter of genetics. But fast forward a decade, and I am running long distances, doing yoga, singing, and playing guitar. I practiced every night, and I got results. In school, then, I was no smarter than the athletic and creative kids. They just spent their evenings and weekends practicing different skills.

Intelligence is a process of learning. You can undertake this process to do something that serves you or something that doesn't. You can use your intelligence to fuel chronic anxiety and self-criticism, or you can use it to understand yourself better. The choice is yours. Don't let your ideas about what you can do keep you from trying. And don't sell yourself short just because other people didn't (or don't) see your potential. You don't need to treat yourself as poorly as you've been treated. With a bit of curiosity, you can untangle yourself from the web of others' expectations and judgments.

If you've ever heard a song lyric or a quote and thought, "Wow, that's true," then you've become aware of your inner conversation. Perhaps you didn't realize what it was. Perhaps you thought you had recognized a universal truth about everyone always. But the universe is gigantic, you know, and absolute truths are hard to come by. When you feel that something is true, you recognize some part of your experience. Each feeling is an opportunity to learn about yourself. Take it.

Curing the Addiction to Certainty

Every answer you have received throughout your life—including any answer you find in this book—is a gift. During the holidays, our friends, relatives, and co-workers give us gifts that end up collecting dust in our attics. Likewise, intellectual gifts can end up cluttering our mental attics. Hoarding isn't only for possessions. We can hoard ideas as well.

Sometimes, we hoard out of guilt, thinking we need to keep certain gifts to make other people happy. We wear ugly sweaters as much as we adopt our parents' belief systems. Other times, we hoard gifts out of shame, thinking we will someday become good enough to use them. We do this with pants that are too small as much as expert opinions about our distress.

How can we declutter those mental attics? How can we separate the useful and meaningful from the rest? We could try contemplating our relationship to the person who first gave us the answer. But a giver's intent does not dictate the value of a gift. If someone takes the time to handmake you a present, then even if it's ugly, you'll likely appreciate it and keep it. However, the same person could give you a handful of peanuts without knowing about your allergy. The intention might be pure, but you'll have no time for gratitude in the midst of anaphylactic shock. Another person could give you a loaf of bread to misdirect you and steal your wallet. But if your wallet is empty and you haven't eaten for days, this ill-intentioned gift will be most welcome. A gift's value depends on your relationship to not only the giver but also the gift itself.

Some presents excite you. Others offend you. But your immediate reaction to a gift doesn't always last. Some gifts grow on you. Others get old. A few turn catastrophic. The relationship between you and any gift you receive (including any intellectual gift) is ever-changing. That which is useless today could become useful tomorrow, and vice versa.

Perhaps you have heard stories like this one: someone buys a painting or a vinyl record for 50 cents at a garage sale, discovers it's an antique, and sells it for thousands. Clearly, the original owner didn't undervalue such a rare item on purpose. Looking at these kinds of situations, we could advocate for the benefits of keeping things and throwing them out only after much deliberation—just in case. Then, there are hoarders: people who accumulate storehouses of every little belonging that crosses their path—just in case. Aesthetics aside, hoarding can be dangerous. The more you amass, the more can go awry. Your possessions can spoil, collapse, or go up in smoke. This seems to make a good case for accumulating as little as possible.

To confuse and complicate matters even more, your relationship to each gift in your attic is not the only relationship that matters. Each physical gift also has a relationship to the Earth. This determines how much waste it would produce if you threw it out. Each gift also has a relationship to the economy and to all the potential future owners of that gift—including you. There are hundreds of relevant relationships to consider. It is just as difficult to make rules about which ideas to believe and which ones to ignore. You might feel that some answer is right in a given moment, but what about how that answer relates to your future self? Should you do what feels good today (because you might die at any moment), or should you delay gratification (to invest in your future)? And what about how each answer relates to your family, your culture, your friends? There are countless dynamics to consider. How can you ever make decisions?

We want rules about how to declutter our minds, declutter our lives. Yet rules are quick fixes. They are static. And, as we keep learning, reality is dynamic. We grasp for static things—ideas as much as material possessions—desperately trying to control the larger patterns that eat us for breakfast. We yearn for certainty. We run from confusion. Some people engage in retail therapy, buying new things to make themselves feel more secure, and others engage in knowledge therapy, amassing new ideas to make themselves feel like they know something. We consume for comfort. We rely on certainty to shield us from the pain of confusion. The truth is staggering, colossal, unfathomable, so we cling to our bite-sized lies. We organize knowledge into bulleted lists and line graphs while the wisdom of the present moment sits patiently at the doors of our perception.

Tackling a messy attic can be just as problematic as filling it. It can also be just as necessary. *What* we do isn't nearly as important as *why* we do it. Buying a couch to fill an emotional void is nothing like buying a couch because you need something to sit on. Throwing out your couch as a substitute for deeper change is different from throwing out your couch because it's moldy. Same couch. Doing something because it's helpful in a given moment is a whole other thing from doing it because it makes you feel like you're in control.

What if, instead of seeking certainty in your decisions and ideas, you became certain of the ever-changing nature of reality? What if each gift, intellectual and otherwise, was as welcome to enter as it was to leave? What if you could entertain each idea, any idea, without making a final decision about whether to hold on to it or let it go?

Suppose that you receive a blender, and you don't need one. You could hold onto it until you find a more suitable owner, until your blender breaks, or until you have an opportunity to sell it. Or you could give it to a friend who doesn't have one. Or you could donate it to a local soup kitchen. There is no right way to relate to a blender! There is only the way you *do* relate to it. And there is no way to know which parts of that relationship you're neglecting or how it will change over time. Even if there was a universally correct choice you could make in every situation, you could never know if you'd made it. Uncertainty hugs our every decision like the stratosphere hugs the Earth. It is as crucial a part of human existence as oxygen. You can never become smart enough to erase all doubt, so why try? Throw out your pens. Write your answers in pencil. Keep an eraser nearby.

If you receive a piece of advice, you don't need to reject it, but you also don't need to accept it as the ultimate truth. You can acknowledge this advice as one way to approach a situation. You could try it out in your life. Maybe it will come in useful, maybe not. In any case, you can remain open to its being useful at any moment. You can seek out people who would benefit from this advice—not so you can preach it at them, but so you can better understand how the world works (and not only how it works for you).

Decluttering is not a weekend spring clean, though it can certainly include one. After all, you could clear out years of amassed possessions only to make space for future hoarding. True decluttering is a state of mind where you step back from all your possessions—material and intellectual—and become open to their arrival and departure. To live free of right answers, you must live free of wrong ones as well. Instead of stockpiling some ideas as permanent parts of your mentality while labelling others as unacceptable intrusions, you can fall open and trust. As Shunryu Suzuki said, "Leave your front door and your back door open." Do not lock anything out, but do not keep anything in. In the world of ideas as much as material things, each object and thought will prove its longevity simply by its longevity. There is no need for a rubric to determine usefulness or meaning because only the useful and the meaningful will be able to remain in the long term. Even the idea of keeping both doors open is not a fixed rule that you are to impose upon reality. Once you try this kind of living, the experience will be its own proof.

Think of an action like sleeping. At least once a day, for most of us, sleep becomes the right thing to do without much effort. If you ignore this need for too long, then the message will knock louder and louder at your door until you receive it (or until it bangs the door down). After we fulfill this need, we receive mental, emotional, and physical rewards—also without effort. Sleep, then, regularly proves itself as a valuable answer to the question "What should I do right now?" The proof is in the experience.

To overcome our addiction to certainty, we don't need to attack the static (or ignore our cravings for it). Rather, we can invite the dynamic. After all, there is nothing wrong with desiring durability or comfort. We want sturdiness from material objects as much as intellectual ideas. Who wants to buy a couch that will disintegrate in a year or two? Who wants to believe in something that will prove useless next week? We want our beliefs like we want our possessions: reliable, functional, resilient. Meanwhile, we buy items only because they are on sale, and we take on ideas only because some expert convinced us of them. We want durability, but we act out of haste. We want long-term benefits, but we seek short-term solutions. We speak so loudly, but we forget to listen.

There are many opportunities to listen, and there are many opportunities to stop listening. Imagine that you needed to buy a bed. You could sabotage yourself by buying the cheapest one without trying it. However, you could also spend months choosing carefully but sabotage yourself nonetheless. After all, you cannot prepare for everything. What if, a few months after your purchase, your back began to hurt? You could tell yourself that, because you put so much time and effort into selecting the perfect one, it could not possibly be your mattress. You could ignore the feedback offered by your experience. Finding a comfortable bed, like finding a useful belief system, is a dynamic process. You can learn to choose more wisely, but you must also continue to evaluate your choices.

Your task is not to separate the correct answers from the wrong ones. You don't need to lie in the grass looking at the night sky and sort the bad stars from the good. All stars are just stars. All answers are just answers. You don't need to put walls around the *in*effective to access that which *is* effective. If you open your mind and remain aware as the answers come and go, only the most useful ones can remain. Ideas that accord with your experience will prove resilient. There's a reason it takes multi-million dollar budgets to sell carbonated drinks, while water sells without a marketing team. The truth endures.

Your task is to look carefully. Observe fully. Begin where you are. If you feel overwhelmed by the task of observing fully and beginning where you are, begin there. Observe that. Which answers come to mind? If you think, "I don't know, I'm confused," then observe that. Do you have a tendency to say you don't know and wait for someone to give a better answer? How does this affect you?

Or maybe you think there's no point in trying because you will not be able to finish. Observe that. Is this a frequent reaction? How does it impact your life? Do you always believe these thoughts?

Or maybe you are pushing yourself into action, looking for something concrete to do. Start observing that. Do you always rush yourself? Do you often try to speed through learning? Do you try to impose a certain pace onto yourself, and could your natural pace be different?

The measure of self-awareness is not *what* you observe but the *act* of observation. Simply by looking, you complete your task. Start where you are. Self-awareness begins the moment you realize it can begin.

Stressful or emotional situations are like the band that a nurse puts around your arm to bring your veins to the surface. The veins are there, but the extra pressure makes them more accessible. When someone upsets you, you have thoughts about that person as well as that situation and your role in it. Allow yourself to become fascinated with the questions and answers that fill your mind in the depths of emotion. Look carefully. Watch your mind's automatic responses. Watch how those responses make you feel. Keep looking. You have been running into squalid back alleys with your blindfold on. It's time to open your eyes and look around. The truth will reveal itself.

The more you allow yourself to see, the more you can allow experience to teach you. Experience will show you what you need today and how that differs from what you needed yesterday. Experience will separate the useless answers from the useful ones. Experience will cleanse away your addiction to experts, quick fixes, static ideas, and—most importantly of all—certainty. Experience must teach you this. I cannot. No book, expert, or guide can make you master this. No doctrine can instill self-awareness within you. Let reality be your teacher.

With open eyes and an open mind, you will develop wisdom about yourself, about people, about life. Knowledge can never compete with such wisdom. Once you drink the fresh truth of experience, you will return to it—even if you go back kicking and screaming. If self-awareness is as nourishing for you as I have found it is for me, you will sell it to yourself.

Conscious Listening

Only the hand that erases can write the true thing.

MEISTER ECKHART

✖ ✖ ✖ ✖ ✖ ✖ ✖ ✖

In our conversations with ourselves as well as with others, miscommunication is omnipresent. It is also covert. Misunderstanding is the snake that crawls into your shoes at night. The tick that latches onto your ankle and paralyzes you. The berry that looks edible but courses with poison. An explorer needs as much passion as caution. Before setting off on a jungle trek, you can research dangerous animals and poisonous plants. Knowledge will not make you immune, but it will make you better prepared. Anticipation helps. Likewise, before you enter into any conversation—as a listener or a participant—you can bring along an awareness of potential misunderstandings. Thus, you can do your best to listen to what is happening beyond what appears to be. To cope with the dangers around us as well as within us, we can accept them and learn from them.

Before we explore how you misunderstand yourself, let us begin with how we misunderstand one another. Let's use the word "conversation." What does this word mean? Two people moving their mouths in turn, making occasional eye contact, matching smiles, occasionally touching—this is a conversation. Who would doubt that?

What about two people moving their mouths simultaneously, matching grimaces, and raising their voices? Is this a conversation? Most people would agree—it is a hostile one but a conversation nonetheless.

Then there are these two people: one is struggling to speak through tears while the other sits in stone-cold silence without making eye contact. Is this a conversation? Some would say not. Some would insist that a conversation happens between two engaged, attentive people. What would you say?

What about a person in an empty room speaking to her reflection? Is this a conversation? And what about a person speaking to himself in an empty room with no mirror in sight? What about a person sitting with her eyes closed under a weeping willow, listening to its leaves blowing in the wind? Is this a conversation? What about a bee lured to a flower by the sweet smell of its pollen?

The trouble with asking you if these are conversations is that your definition of the word "conversation" could be different from mine. But why must that be? Surely, we could consult the dictionary. We could. But any definition is a combination of words—each with a definition for us to disagree about. Of course, we could continue to search for those words in the dictionary as well. Thus, we would spin ourselves into a useless web. This confusion is most notable with abstract concepts such as wisdom, truth, and reality. The dictionary will tell you that reality is what's real, what's real is what's true, the truth is what's true, and what's true is what's real.

But suppose that, regardless of these obstacles, you and I decided to consult the dictionary anyway. Let's say we found a definition, set it on the table between us, and looked at it. Each word in that definition would open a mental door to a room of associations, emotions, and experiences. Since such doors exist within each of our separate minds, the rooms they lead to will, inevitably, differ. We would look at the same thing but see something different. Thus, you could continue to defend your interpretation, and I could do the same. We could find proof for our own theories and discard the rest. Worse yet, we could both be trying to say the same thing but remain blind to this fact because of the meanings we attach to the words we use and hear. We could become very annoyed with each other like this.

Sometimes, it seems like we're on the same page. For example, I could point to the sun, look at you, and say "sun." You would nod and agree. Yes, this is the sun. But what if you speak Russian? I would point and say "sun." You would say "solntse." We could get into a fight about it, but likely, we wouldn't. We'll probably understand that we are using different words to describe the same thing. But what about a word like "love"? We cannot point to anything. We use this word to represent a complex system of memories, emotions, and ideas. I cannot see inside your mind, and you cannot see inside mine. There is no way for us to know exactly what each other experiences when we say "love." Or "justice." Or even "trampoline."

You already accept that you do not understand someone who speaks a foreign language. Yet we all have a mental dictionary we use to translate the significance of words and events. We all speak our own native tongue.

Misunderstanding is a fact of life. To some degree, you no doubt misunderstand yourself as well as the people around you. And those people, in turn, misunderstand you—some of them occasionally, most of them ceaselessly. This is not something we can cure. However, when we bring awareness to these patterns, we can accept misinterpretation as an invitation to understand rather than disagree.

Some years ago, I would debate about the word "God." I would say, "God does not exist." When I said this, I pictured a man in the sky who passed judgment on everyone below. To me, this was illogical. How could there be such a man? Growing up in the Ukraine, dropping this belief was easy. No one around me believed in God except my grandmother. She believed. And she kept telling me about Him. As a child, I tried to believe. When I grew up, I couldn't. As I solidified my beliefs, I began to judge hers. How could this woman—an educated, intelligent doctor with grey hair—have believed in a man in the sky? I could not understand her. Now, many years after her death, I think I do, but who knows? All I knew were her words and facial expressions. All I knew were her behaviours and gestures as they related to *my* behaviours and gestures. I'd always been ignorant of the rest. Maybe I understand her now. Maybe I do not. This is the reality of human communication.

Some people say they don't believe in God, but they believe in an energy that moves through all living things. Others say they do believe in God, and they claim that God is an energy moving through all living things. Some people believe in a holy book, and their faith gives them the same feeling of certainty that sustains people of other faiths as well as non-believers. Over this, we start wars.

Understanding is the heart of language—the purpose of it. When we don't keep this essential purpose in mind, communication degenerates. Language becomes a vessel for misunderstanding.

I judged my grandmother's beliefs and wondered about her ability to see things as they are. In fact, she simply didn't see things the same way I did. She talked about a man in the sky, which gave her some feeling. I imagine that it now gives me a similar feeling to perceive the interconnected nature of the universe. Maybe this is true. Maybe it is not. I will never know. Even if she were still alive, I might never know. There is no quick and easy way to get on the same page with another person. All communication is an act of faith. If only we acknowledged the incredible amount of trust we put in each other every time we speak— trust that we will do our best to understand—then we might stop breaking it as often as we do.

We think that we hear each other. We think that, when we speak, people understand us. We think that, when we listen, we understand what other people say. But we usually don't. When we have felt something fall through our fingers—when we've smelled it, tasted it, danced with it—we might relate to someone who is trying to tell us about that same thing. But even then, we will only understand that person's mindset as much as it reflects our own. You and I may empathize with one another and discover a significant overlap of experience, yet our overlap does not define our entire relationship. And our perception of that overlap is bound to differ, even if we do not acknowledge those differences. If we are so limited in our ability to understand people with similar experiences, then imagine how little we understand everyone else.

But we try to understand. Don't we? Don't we do our best to understand each other despite this constant rift between what we see and what others see, what we see and what we say, what we do and what we feel? Don't we try our best to grasp the intended meanings of other people's words? Or do we default to expecting their symbols to be identical to ours? Do we listen consciously—with the intention to understand—or do we unconsciously seek to reinforce what we already believe is true?

Think of how negatively you react to certain words that people use to describe you. And how high you get on compliments that reflect the way you'd like others to perceive you. And how difficult it is to accept compliments that you don't believe are true. *Are* you looking for a way to understand better? Or are you clutching for shreds of what you already think you know?

Conscious listening begins with accepting that, no matter how well-read or well-spoken we are, we all struggle with understanding others and making ourselves understood. The words we use to represent our experience will never be the experience itself. The word "rock" will never be a rock. The word "love" will never be our experience of what we call love. The journey of understanding begins with admitting that we rarely do. Because we communicate with symbols, we don't say exactly what we see or express exactly what we mean. We also don't communicate about all our experiences. Sometimes, we don't have the words to describe them. Other times, we're ashamed. But most of the time, we simply don't notice.

There is so much we do not see, cannot see, about ourselves, about other people, about the world. We can't see x-rays with our naked eyes. We can't see infrared. Even with the parts of reality we *can* access, we see selectively. We formulate stories about the world and see only as much as our narratives allow. Even if we try to "be present"—as the gurus advise us to do—we can only attend to so much at once.

Take a moment to look around you. Everything has a texture, a shape, a taste, a smell. Everything elicits its own arsenal of memories, associations, and definitions. Everything looks different up close than it does from afar. Everything has a unique place in your life story. Now, notice your bodily sensations: the clothing touching your skin, this book in your hands, the temperature of your environment. Then, notice your thoughts and feelings: the worries, the hopes, the to-do list, the daydreams, the insecurities. Think of the vast reality of each moment. Could you always be 100% open to all of that? Could you function if you tried to experience every single part of the world around you? Could you be open to the evolution of every single new possibility in every single second?

Through our vital efforts to organize and prioritize reality, we distort it. Then, when we share our experiences of that distortion, we miscommunicate about them! We cannot remove our tendency to misunderstand. But we *can* learn to become more aware, to look deeper, to listen more consciously. Of course, we still will not be able to see *everything*, but we can learn to see *more*. Thus, we can understand better.

We can learn to allow multiple answers to the same question, and we can learn to ask more questions instead of clinging to our beliefs. Before you thought you knew the definition of each word you now use, you wondered what it meant. The questions that lead to understanding are already within you, hiding beneath the hoarded answers.

Children face each day with questions, with wonder. They ask, "What's going on?" They ask, "What does it mean?" As we grow older, we begin to make the dangerous assumption that we know what's happening—that we know the final answers to these questions. And when we don't know, we assume that we *should*. Instead of giving our inner questions the space they deserve, we learn to answer them automatically, and we feel shame each time we're unable to answer quickly enough. We lose our wonder. Thus, we lose our ability to understand.

What if you allowed your childhood curiosity to re-emerge from underneath layers of adult know-how? What if you tried to look beyond your preferred symbols, your definitions, your inner dictionary? What if you took the time to question your assumptions about how other people define their words? What if you tried to excavate the intended meanings of other people's communications?

Imagine if you calmly said to an infant: "I hate you." The child would blink back at you, unaffected. But if *I* said the same to *you*, your reaction would be different. You would look up my words in your inner dictionary, conclude what I meant by them, and become upset with me. But what if I had no way to express to you that I felt unloved by you? What if the only way I could show you my feelings was to make you feel the same? What if I said I hated you to express that your words or actions made me feel like *you* hate *me*? Of course, I would be the one with the communication problem. But imagine that I was open to learning new ways to articulate my emotions, and you were open to listening for my meaning instead of only looking up the words I say in your internal lexicon? Like this, we could really go somewhere. We could transform our relationship. We would still misunderstand each other, no doubt, but we could become more compassionate, intimate, and loving with one another by acknowledging and integrating our tendency to miscommunicate.

When a person focuses on his or her understanding of a situation while ignoring the validity of others' viewpoints, conflict arises. Peace, on the other hand, requires flexibility. To pacify our relationship, we need to explore each other's perspectives. To invite new information. To ask, "How can I understand you better?"

Imagine that reality is a boulder in a wide-open field. You and I are looking at this rock, walking around it, seeing various parts of it. Sometimes, we are on opposite sides, seeing two different perspectives. Other times, we are on the same side, perhaps even looking at the same spot, yet our perceptions still differ. Maybe you are more interested in the bugs crawling around the boulder, whereas I am more interested in the moss. We are bound to see differently. If we listen to one another, however, this can be an advantage rather than a hindrance. If I let you tell me about the bugs, and you let me talk about the moss, and then we both decide to explore each other's curiosities, we will have formed a more holistic understanding of this stone together.

We do not need to erase our assumptions, prejudices, or biases. We must simply learn to expand our awareness beyond them. For every word in this book, you have a mental definition. For every experience in your life, you assume its causes. This is unavoidable. And it isn't actually harmful. For each question, you think of some answer first. The trick is to keep looking, keep asking, keep wondering.

Most of us seek to replace our questions with answers. After we reach the first reasonable conclusion about someone's intended meaning, we stop asking, "What is she trying to say?" After we discover a definition of the word "conversation," we stop asking, "What does it mean?" This seems harmless in the moment, but it is incompatible with conscious listening. To listen holistically, we must allow our questions to coexist with their potential answers. And we must allow our paradoxical answers and hypocritical questions to coexist as well. Awareness is a journey of addition, not subtraction. To see clearly, we must welcome the validity of every perspective.

In any situation, we can notice our automatic, firm, robotic answers and say, "Yes, that could be. What else could be?" We can observe our first impressions, our reasonable conclusions, our acceptable explanations and say, "Yes, this is, but what else is?" We can notice our assumptions and kindly, gently (and perhaps with a spoonful of

69

humour) say, "Okay, there's that, and what else?" And when we find ourselves asking questions that we don't have answers for, we can say, "I don't know," or "I don't know, but let's explore that." In each moment, you can ask, "How can I understand better?" You could ask this question hundreds of times every day for the rest of your life, and it would not be too much. The more you practice this, the less you will feel like you know; yet the closer you will be to the truth.

Instead of perceiving confusion as a pesky intruder, let it play within the walls of your consciousness. Let it colour the walls and seep into the floorboards. The less energy you devote to removing uncertainty, the more energy you can devote to accepting it. By allowing confusion, you create fertile ground for curiosity. This is not the same curiosity that has moved you through the marketing funnels of various gurus. When curiosity is a means to an end—when we seek answers only to ease our discomfort—it reinforces our unconsciousness. When curiosity is an end in itself—a perspective, a viewpoint, a way of life—then it fuels an easy, egoless, playful relationship between ourselves and the world around us. The less you demand to know, the more you will understand. This understanding will not be a mountain peak of final knowledge but an active climb to a peak that might not exist. The quest for truth is never over.

To understand, you must keep questioning, keep digging, keep searching for new perspectives. Some people might call this overthinking. However, there is a difference between desperately seeking certainty and slowly expanding your vision to include more of the world around you. Overthinking is about running around in circles, thinking the same old anxiety-provoking thoughts, feeling the same old emotions while you slowly lose touch with reality. Conscious listening is about soaring to the heights and plummeting to the depths so that you can be at one with how things are.

These may look identical to the casual observer. The difference is in the experience.

Conscious listening will allow you to perceive parts of reality that your mind has been ignoring. Because they contradict your opinions. Because they do not conform to your story of what is happening. Listening is also a transferable skill. Trying to understand other people will help you understand yourself, and vice versa. You'll learn to seek out the depths of meaning in each piece of communication instead of merely judging the clothes in which it arrives. Conscious listening will pry open your mind. But do not take my word for it. Invite this habit to be a guest in your life and remain aware of how it affects you. If it is useful, it will prove itself.

Let us practice our new habit by returning to the word "conversation." According to my definition, each of the scenarios at the start of this chapter is a conversation. If you disagree, then likely, you and I assign different meanings to this word. So now, you have the opportunity to expand your awareness to include mine. You do not need to give up your existing definition. Instead of perceiving our views as either/or, you can see them as and/and. You see something different from what I see, and you can *add* my perspective to yours. Our understanding is cumulative, not zero-sum.

In this book, I use the word "conversation" to describe dynamic relationships. You have an ever-changing relationship with everything and everyone around you: with your reflection, your family, and your coffee table. You also have relationships within you: between your mind and body, your heart and liver, your self-judgment and self-love. The outside world is composed of such relationships as well: between the bee and the flower, the ocean and the mountain, the atmosphere and outer space.

71

A conversation is a unit that we can break down into smaller patterns and assimilate into larger ones. We can zoom in to observe your inner conversation: the world of interrelated patterns under your skin. We can zoom in further to observe certain "voices" inside you: the patterns themselves. We can zoom in even more to find conversations inside those voices: the interrelated patterns within patterns. We can also zoom out to observe your conversations with other people: the dynamics in your human relationships. Then, we can zoom out even more to observe the conversation of life: the mysterious and interconnected Universe.

Your inner conversation connects you to all of existence. Like an intricate web, everything within you interrelates and interconnects with the outside world. If we poke just one fibre of the web with a tiny branch, the entire structure shifts. Each element in the web of life is like a note in a symphony. It does not and cannot exist by itself. Even if a single note stands alone in a solo, it reintegrates into the whole moments later. And it always remains a part of the piece. Each note is unique. Each note makes a difference. And, still, each note's identity is inseparable from its role in the concerto. The notes entwine into patterns that are as predictable as they are creative. Each note echoes, contrasts, and magnifies the others. This is the music of life.

As you listen to yourself, you will begin to hear life's song. When you do, you might think it is beautiful. Reality is intricate, multi-dimensional, and complex. It is ever-present and ever-changing. Every moment we spend observing this pattern leads us to a truth so encompassing that it dissolves our illusory detachment from the rest of existence. There is something bigger going on here, and we are all part of it. There is something deeply healing about this realization.

Life's conversation can also be frightening, ironically for the same reasons it is beautiful. It is *so* big, *so* complex, and *so* intricate, we feel paralyzed by our smallness. We feel limited by our perceptions. We feel dwarfed by our lack of knowledge. The truth is an ocean, and we have but a spoon. This can be frightening, yes, but it can also be humbling. Because why else would it scare you to realize that you cannot know everything unless you believe, somewhere deep inside, that you do?

Understanding requires curiosity and humility. We can hear more, see clearer, and understand better; but we cannot hear, see, or know it all. And we don't need to. Our task is not to decipher the complexities of the entire universe but only to live more harmoniously within it. To play in an orchestra, we need not master every instrument. We must simply learn to play our own. But first, we must learn to hear the music.

So as you voyage into your inner conversation, you go armed with an important tool: conscious listening. Instead of a map, it gives you a compass. Instead of giving a static answer, it asks a dynamic question.

The Voices Within

*Pull out from the depths those thoughts that you
do not understand, and spread them out in the
sunlight and know the meaning of them.*

E.M. FORSTER

✖ ✖ ✖ ✖ ✖ ✖ ✖

Conventional wisdom says, "Follow your dreams." For most of my life, I've tried to follow mine in the conventional sense—by bringing my fantasies to life. This was not always such a wise idea.

As a child, I began to dream about performing on various stages. I'd dream of singing my heart out, accepting the Nobel Peace Prize, and giving an Oscar acceptance speech. I wanted to be an actress, a politician, a talk show host, and a ballerina. These daydreams were once so powerful and mesmerizing that I'd often find myself mid-laugh, mid-Oscar-winning-smile, or mid-passionate-political-roar in public places. These moments embarrassed me, but they also motivated me. I strove to fulfill these passions, both as a child and as an adult. While some people accused me of flushing my potential down the toilet, I believe that my quest to bring these dreams to reality was harmless (and even valuable). But these were not the only dreams I had.

In grade 7, four years after immigrating to Canada, I began to have a recurring daydream. It went something like this. I pull up in front of my elementary school in a red sports car driven by some sexy man. All my grade 7 classmates happen to be standing on the front lawn. I gracefully hop out of the car to go pick something up at the principal's office. I am now a fully-grown adult with perfect breasts and a tiny waist. My stretch marks have disappeared. My skin is tanned, pimple-free, and glowing. Miraculously, I have grown to almost six feet tall. As I walk up to the building, everyone stops and gasps.

"Oh my God! Is that her?!"

They try to talk to me, but no. No. You didn't want me back then, and now that I'm perfect and beautiful, *I* don't want *you*.

The accessories in the story would change. Sometimes, the man was dark-skinned, sometimes light. Sometimes, the car was the one from *Sixteen Candles*; other times, *The Fast and the Furious*. Sometimes, I'd be wearing a slinky dress; other times, shorts. Sometimes, I'd be talking on a cell phone, laughing while my hair blew in the breeze like a shampoo commercial. Sometimes, I'd spring out of the car as it was still moving. In all these scenarios, one thing remained constant: I felt glamorous, important, and compensated—by the jealous stares of my classmates—for the years of taunting and rejection.

I had this dream countless times. It was not until years later that I realized how delusional it truly was. Even if, genetics be damned, I could have grown into a six-foot-tall model, this would have taken years. My grade 7 classmates would have become adults by that time. Even if the school had (for some reason) asked me to return years later, I would have ended up, at best, as a provocatively dressed adult woman strutting in front of a group of gaping children

I'd never met before. This could be called many things, but glamorous is not one of them. To follow this dream would have been inadvisable, to say the least. Yet I tried to fulfill it in other embarrassing ways. I would dress up and strut down the street, imagining the reactions of passersby—reactions that painted my imaginary world over the land-scape of reality.

Then, there were the dark daydreams—the ones that aren't so funny to remember. In elementary school, around the same time, I started having daydreams about getting sick or hurt. I dreamed about going to the hospital, being diagnosed with cancer, breaking my arm, and even dying. I also had dreams about this happening to people I knew. While the scenarios changed like the wind, one plot element remained constant: the phone call. I'd be sitting in class or, as I grew older, at work. I'd answer the phone, listen for a moment, and go ghastly white. Everyone would look at me. Everyone would pity me. In versions of this daydream where I had died, someone who had wronged me would pick up the phone. Gasp. Blanch. Remorse. Later on, all my class-mates, family members, or co-workers would sit in a circle lamenting all the ways they had mistreated me. Driven by these daydreams, I milked every pain and tragedy. I used my wounds as a way to get attention instead of addressing them. Thus, they remained unhealed. I kept myself sick. Worse yet, the more I learned to get attention this way, the less I felt bound to the truth. What began as a bit of exag-geration grew into a convoluted labyrinth of lies.

When I first acknowledged these tendencies, I felt like a disgusting monster. I vowed never to tell anyone about what happened in the dark corners of my mind. I started to think of myself as twisted and sick-minded. This self-image strengthened as I began to have violent daydreams as well. Driven by unresolved anger toward three men who had hurt me, I wove a tapestry of resentment around relationships, love, and men. In my early twenties, I began to have fantasies about going to a bar, having a man disrespect me, and beating him to a bloody pulp. Everyone would look at me. Everyone would fear and respect me. They'd whisper about my strength. These daydreams were just as powerful and consuming. I'd find myself mid-sneer or mid-aggressive-growl in the same public places. These dreams, I also tried to fulfill. With too many drinks in me—which, for a while, I often had—I would see a man doing something I deemed non-consensual, and I would play saviour. Oftentimes, I'd "save" myself. My dreams of strength suffocated my empathy. It was especially unfair to the men in my life whom I pigeonholed as manipulative, violent, and controlling. All the while, the only one who merited those labels was the person I had become.

The daydreams seeped into real life. Before parties and club nights, I would imagine making groups of people laugh. I'd imagine saying the perfect thing to drop jaws and earn respect. I'd imagine the music skipping a beat when I walked in. Just like the movies. Then, every time I stepped into a real-life social situation, I'd imagine people judging me, hating me, ridiculing me. My idealisms so easily turned to paranoia. My only self-protective mechanism was addiction. When I was sober in public, I'd think, "Oh no, everyone is *looking* at me." When I was intoxicated, I'd think, "Oh yeah, everyone is looking at *me!*" For the most part, these things were happening only in my head. My daydream life was spiraling into a nightmare.

Like this, I tried to follow my dreams. But as I grew from a hopeful child who just wanted to be loved into an addicted, paranoid young woman who wanted to hurt and be hurt for attention, "follow your dreams" seemed like dangerous advice. The real danger, however, was my inability to interpret these fantasies. Instead of trying to make all my dreams into reality, I needed to understand them, decode them. To follow them like a private investigator follows a target.

As I began my journey of self-discovery, these daydreams began to disappear. The first to go were the violent ones. With each person I forgave, my anger subsided. My hatred of men evaporated. Then, I began to make eye contact with my reflection as well as with other people. I realized that all eyes were *not* on me.

My dreams of importance held strong for longer. As I was writing *The Love Mindset*, I daydreamed about Oprah calling me while I was at my dreaded day job. She would tell me she loved my book and wanted to fly me to her house for a few days before putting me on the show. These dreams began to disappear when I became a coach. Each time I faced a person heart to heart, soul to soul, I felt important. I'd come off every session with a layer of sweat on my back and butterflies in my stomach. As I learned to be more honest and compassionate, these feelings became even more powerful. With time, my dreams of admiration disappeared. I had satisfied my need for significance in a most unexpected way!

Learning to support and encourage other people also eradicated my fantasies of being better than them. True power, I discovered, was to be powerful *with* others, not *over* them. I experience my power through the connection I feel to each person, each moment. I am no longer stuck in a cave, dreaming of the sky. I have my wings spread. There's no need to create an imaginary world in my head because I have found magic in the one that exists.

I wanted to matter, and now I know I do. I don't have a sports car. I'm not six feet tall. Oprah hasn't called. I know I matter because I feel it when I connect to people, to nature, to life. When I see raw human passion and strength, I feel how much we *all* matter. And when I witness the intricate patterns of the natural world, I feel how much *everything* matters.

What I find most remarkable is this: moments that have most resembled the scenarios in my daydreams have not satisfied me. Such situations only caused my fantasies to persist or intensify. After I received an award onstage as I was graduating college, I fantasized about getting more awards. After I found myself on the set of a local television station talking about my book, I dreamed of doing more TV interviews. But after an intimate chat with my partner or a deep conversation with a client, I dream of nothing. I feel full. When I'm by myself writing, singing, or playing music, I feel satisfied. It seems reasonable to fantasize about food when you're starving, but who would dream about food after having a hearty meal? An addict, that's who. In hindsight, that's exactly what I was.

My fantasies were self-communications coded in my own unique language. But instead of trying to translate them accurately, I made assumptions. I see now that the messages themselves were simple. I wanted to matter, so I dreamed of being on stage. I wanted strength, so I dreamed of violence. I wanted empathy, so I dreamed of being hurt. I wanted love, so I dreamed of being perfect. These desires exist in all human beings, and my mind did its best to construct scenarios where I could fulfill them. But all I had to draw from was too much television and a poverty of real-world experience. Because I misunderstood the language of my daydreams, my unfulfilled desires intensified. So did my fantasies about fulfilling them. Instead of using my daydreams to guide me toward reality, I warped my inner world to match my imaginary one. I became so addicted to my make-believe emotions that real-life experiences could never compete with them. Living without explosive rage was more peaceful, but it did not give me ecstasy. The moments I had with my clients were blissful, but they were not euphoric. The epiphanies that changed my life lit me on fire, but those flames only burned for so long. After a lifetime of extremism and self-deception, I had to get used to peace, to silence, to the real world.

Without violent anger, I no longer felt strong. Without paranoia, I no longer felt confident. Without egotistical delusions, I no longer felt important. Without attention-seeking lies, I no longer knew how to get reactions out of people. I had to learn to meet my emotional needs in other ways—healthier ways. And I had to navigate new relationships with anger, fear, attention, and imagination. It was a difficult journey. It definitely was not a wave of blissful realization peppered with moments of enlightenment and epiphany. It was messy, beautiful, uncomfortable, and meaningful all at once. It was as reality always is.

The more I understood and fulfilled my needs, the more authentically I could relate to the world around me. Men, instead of scapegoats, became human beings—full of the same fears, hopes, doubts, and beauty as everyone else. The stage, instead of a pedestal for admiration, became a place for sharing my emotions and ideas. My creative pursuits, instead of being ploys for attention, became methods of self-expression. My wounds, instead of earning me pity, became pathways to empathy. And my dreams, instead of addictive self-delusions, became guideposts to self-discovery.

I have learned to question my assumptions. I have learned to hear my inner voices and become curious about their intended communications. I have learned to be comfortable with silence. I have learned to match my translations to reality. I have made some progress, but I cannot claim that I've discovered my own Rosetta Stone of correct translations for all my dreams, feelings, and thoughts. Learning to interpret the voices within me has been, and will continue to be, a lifetime job. In the end, the most important thing I have learned is this: my inner experience, even when it shows up to me in the plainest English, is always open for interpretation. My mind already translates my self-communications—with or without my consent. And I can choose to be an active participant in that translation process. I can choose to understand instead of pretending to know.

Lost In Translation

Of all the questions we ask ourselves from day to day, perhaps the most important is "What does this mean?" This simple query is a catalyst between reality and our perception of it. It links what happens to our ideas about what is happening. The way we answer this question governs our relationships—not only with other people but also with our bodies, our thoughts, and our past experiences. It defines how we "listen" to the world: what we focus on, how we interpret what we perceive, and which conclusions we make about how things work. Thus, it determines how we "speak": how we respond to emotional triggers, when we take certain actions, and which words we use to communicate with ourselves and others.

As we explored in the last chapter, our tendency to misunderstand other people comes from our unconscious assumptions about what their words mean. It is the same with the "words" spoken by our minds and bodies. If you are struggling with changing your behaviours, you might be misinterpreting your self-communications.

For example, how do you decide that it's time to eat? Some people consult the clock. Others eat every time they want to taste something delicious. Some only eat when they feel their stomachs rumbling. Others can perceive their glucose levels drop by a few milligrams. And yet others—myself included—misinterpret feelings of loneliness or exhaustion as hunger. I am a recovered binge eater. As the old saying goes, you can't get enough of what you don't need. For most of us, such misunderstandings run rampant. We neglect the body's signals because we misinterpret them. To understand ourselves better, our task remains the same: to observe reality with wide-open eyes, to look beyond the first explanation, to listen more consciously.

Conscious listening is a skill that we must cultivate, practice, and refine. Listening, on the other hand, is a necessity of everyday life. It is an essential prerequisite to all "speech"—that is, all behaviour. Even a person who spends most of the day screaming at the top of his lungs listens to his inner urge to act this way.

We can divide listening into two parts: interpretation and observation. Observation is what you hear, and interpretation is what you understand. If you are listening to someone, you observe her gestures, words, and expressions. Then, you interpret what she means. Before you go to the bathroom, you observe the sensations in your body. Then, you interpret them.

Usually, observation and interpretation seamlessly integrate with one another. Usually, but not always. One instance where you can catch observation alone is when you hear someone speaking in an unfamiliar language. Because you're not in the habit of interpreting that language, your mind goes back to the drawing board: observing. You hear the sounds, see the gestures, feel the energy in the spoken words. Some people only linger here for a second before they jump into wondering, hypothesizing, interpreting. Others observe for longer. The length of the gap differs, but it is a perceptible gap nonetheless. You may experience something similar with animals, babies, or anyone else whose communications you cannot easily understand (or, at least, you cannot easily *tell* yourself you understand). Your patterns of interpretation are like roads. When you have taken a route hundreds of times, you can arrive at your destination without any memory of travelling there. Practice makes your behaviours automatic. When you take a new route, on the other hand, you are more alert and observant.

Another situation where you might notice a similar phenomenon is in a bustling crowd of people. Excessive stimulation often delays interpretation. For some people, the delay is only a few seconds long. They breathe in the chaos, take it all in, and then proceed to their next action or location. For others, the delay is much longer. They feel steadily more overwhelmed until they experience enough pain to elicit one single interpretation: "I have to get out of here." Sensory overload might numb the interpretation reflex, but eventually, it returns and drives us into some kind of action.

As a newborn, you spent more of your time observing than interpreting. The whole world was a giant crowd speaking a foreign language. You observed it with open-minded curiosity. Soon enough, you began to deduce patterns and formulate them into ideas. For example, you figured out that if you cried, your mother would give you milk. You discovered that this milk helped soothe the discomfort in your tummy. If this process was in any way violated—if perhaps your cries were not answered or you did not receive enough food to give you comfort—then you figured out that the world was a confusing place where you might never get what you want. You learned, and you learned fast. You translated the world into your own dialect. Then, you learned to speak, not only to the people around you but also to yourself. Each time your body chattered to you about some pain or pleasure, you listened and responded. Over time, you developed a complex, multi-layered conversation within yourself as well as with your environment.

This is how you have developed all your automatic patterns from walking to worrying. You have practiced some interpretations and responses so many times that they've become second nature. This kind of learning is helpful for skills such as reading, walking, and writing. Our ability to perform complex behaviours on autopilot is undoubtedly responsible for much of human achievement. Yet there is a dark side to our acumen. Our self-destructive habits as much as our people-pleasing ones can become just as habitual, just as automatic.

No matter how immovable some habit feels to you now, it started once upon a time with some meaningless observation. You can trace any limp to some pain or discomfort, and you can trace each emotional defense mechanism to some unpleasant reaction. You can trace every word now you say to some word you once heard. These processes are often unconscious, but this can change. There is a cosmic difference between being unaware and being unable to be aware.

We observe, then we interpret, then we act. We listen, then we translate, then we speak. We can do much to influence this process. We can learn to observe for longer and translate better. We can learn to become aware of our interpretation patterns, question them, and change them. However, we cannot *avoid* interpretation, no matter how self-aware we are. We must translate what we observe. This is not good or bad. This is simply the way things are. Interpretation is like a pane of glass between you and the world.

That glass is there. It must be there. You can, however, choose whether you will clean it or let it collect dust while you make up stories about why the world is so dirty.

A window does not become grimy overnight. It accumulates a little bit of dust each day. Likewise, misunderstanding is a cumulative process. You observe something meaningless, interpret it, and act on it. Then, you observe that action, interpret it, and take further actions. This process goes on and on. If you are unaware of your interpretations, you are likely to tell yourself inaccurate stories about why you do certain things. For example, you might often feel irritated with a roommate and snap at him. You might claim that he annoys you on purpose. But what if he subconsciously reminds you of your father, and the irritation is pointing out your unhealed resentment? Without questioning your interpretations, you cannot heal.

Imagine that you are reading a book in a foreign language, translating the words as you go. Around chapter one, you accidentally translate "should" as "cannot." Your misunderstanding begins to snowball. You are not aware of this. You just keep trying to make sense of what you are reading. One sentence says, "Mark should have turned left, but he didn't." You read it as saying, "Mark cannot have turned left, but he didn't." You spin your wheels trying to understand. Eventually, you come up with an explanation. You deduce that somebody prohibited Mark from turning left, but this was unnecessary because he never turned left anyway. This translation is nonsense, but you could believe it just enough to keep reading. Until the next time you encounter the word "should." Your frustration might lead you to question yourself: "Am I awful at reading this language?" Or you might question the book: "Is it poorly written? Is the author incompetent?" Your frustration, however, has a different message. This feeling is not giving you feedback on your abilities or the book's worth. It is communicating about your errone-ous translation of one little word. Learning to recognize when your inner windows are dirty is a crucial skill.

Mistranslation is a notorious cause of relationship troubles—a silent assassin that hides in the folds of our shirts while we blame our partners or blame ourselves. Imagine a woman who gets an occasional feeling: a longing. She interprets it as a desire for her partner's attention. Then, she becomes vigilant about what her partner is focusing on and grows resentful when she finds him or her attending to something (or someone) else. Even if her partner makes a diligent effort to fulfill her needs, it will never be enough. No one else can read her desires at the exact moment she has them. She will never be truly satisfied. But what is happen-ing here? Must her feeling mean "I need my partner to pay attention to me"? Or could it simply mean "I need atten-tion"? These interpretations might sound the same, but there is a world of difference between the two. If you as-sume that you need attention from some specific person, you will miss valuable opportunities to get it from other people—most notably, from yourself!

Such misunderstandings also come in the form of "I want him to tell me I'm beautiful," or "I want her to tell me I've done the right thing." These are interpretations of feel-ings. The feelings themselves do not specify who must de-liver them. We could interpret those same desires as "I want to feel beautiful," and "I want to feel like I've done the right thing." In one case, we assume that a certain person must give us some feeling. In the other case, we simply notice a need for the feeling itself. The more you can identify your desires without attaching them to deliverers, the more you will be able to hear and influence your inner conversation. This does not only apply to people. We block the path to our raw desires with material things, such as money and status symbols. We obstruct it with future events, such as marriage, accomplishments, and apologies. The more roadblocks there are in your interpretations, the more traffic jams you will have inside your mind. You will be unable to remove that desire, yet unable to fulfill it. You will be stuck. But your immobility will be neither an inherent state nor a result of external circumstances. It will be a by-product of chronic misinterpretation.

Discovering your mistranslations can help you excavate unmet needs. Once you feed your hunger, you will better understand your symptoms of starvation. This can lead to profound self-forgiveness. You can dive into your most harmful tendencies, find the core needs that fuel them, and learn to fulfill those needs in healthier ways. Thus, you can establish sustainable patterns of self-care. As you engage in daily self-nourishment, you will become less vulnerable to promises of quick fixes and magical solutions. A well-fed person is hard to seduce. Becoming curious about your self-communications can give you precious insight into what you've labelled as senseless annoyances or terminal defects. It can liberate you from the discouraging struggle of trying to remove your so-called problems. Imagine how different your life could be if you committed to discovering the reasons for your reactions rather than always trying to augment them.

Your task is to question your translations—to wipe off the pane of glass between you and the world. Yet every time you do this, you acknowledge that glass. You can question your interpretations, but you cannot transcend them. The way you look at the world, even if you look at it as consciously as possible, will never define the world. No matter how true some idea sounds, it cannot be the truth itself. Any idea is only a photocopy of the untouchable, incomprehensible reality within which you are a guest. Still, some photo-copies are more accurate than others.

Every book you've ever read, including this one, has undergone at least two translations: the author converts ideas into words, and you decipher meaning. When a book undergoes a third adaptation (namely, transcription into a foreign language), the potential for misinterpretation increases even more. The Tao Te Ching, for example, has been translated hundreds of times. Its original language, Classical Chinese, lacks punctuation and relies on long-ago contexts to communicate meaning. The identity of the author (or authors) is a mystery. The bamboo strips containing the original text are corrupted and difficult to read. On top of this, the book is full of ambiguous wordplay! Translation, in short, is difficult. Nevertheless, suppose that we could see inside people's minds, living or dead. We could look inside the author. Then, we could look inside the readers. For each version of the book, we could compare these images. Out of a few hundred translations, some would do better at expressing Lao Tzu's intended communication to a majority of readers. Thus, while no translation can ever be the original, some translations must be better than others at transmitting the original meaning. Of course, we can only hypothesize about which ones they are; yet hypothesizing is a valuable practice. Just because we can never be sure that we've found the truth doesn't mean it's not worth seeking.

The practice of self-awareness is a lifelong search for truth. It is like consulting a dictionary to check for translation errors, but instead of referring to a book, you refer to your experience. Every time you hear a word—whether it is spoken by your spouse or your left leg—you can observe your immediate translations and ponder other possibilities. And every time you catch yourself doing something harmful—whether it is smoking or worrying—you can try to separate your observations from your interpretations. In any situation, you can ask, "What am I observing?" and "How am I translating it?" And most importantly, "Is my translation accurate?"

You might wonder: "How can I know if I've learned to understand better?" Once again, you must let experience be your teacher. For example, imagine that you move to France without learning a word of French. Every morning, on your way out the door, your neighbour says something to you. You believe he is saying something rude and uncalled for—perhaps swearing at you—so you do not respond. One day, you have an epiphany that, maybe, your neighbour has been greeting you all along! You decide to test your theory. At the next opportunity, after he says his usual incomprehensible line, you smile and wave. How do you know if you have interpreted accurately? You know by his reaction. The proof is in the experience.

The Characters in Your Inner Drama

Remember a time when you walked into a room of people and got an uneasy feeling. Where did you assume this feeling was coming from? Maybe you thought it was your intuition. Or maybe you assumed it was anxiety. Or self-judgment. Or introversion. Maybe you have experienced all these interpretations at different points in your life. The feeling itself could be identical, but your assumption about its origins changes your interpretation, and thus, your reaction.

Nothing you feel is random. No experience is without a cause. As they say, everything happens for a reason. This doesn't mean that what happens is inevitable. It means, simply, that every event has a past, a future, and a relationship to everything else. For each word you speak to yourself—whether it is a pain, a dream, or a desire—there is an underground network of causes and effects. Our search for meaning, then, must go beyond individual words. Trying to find mistranslations word by word is like trying to learn a language by reading the dictionary. You don't speak word by word. You speak in sentences, stories, anecdotes. You understand (and misunderstand) in patterns.

Imagine that your inner conversation is a movie script. If you remove all the character names, the words become a meaningless mess. Of course, on some level, everything *is* a meaningless mess. This is important to keep in mind. But while nothing has inherent *meaning*, everything does have a *relationship* to everything else. You can better understand your symptoms, emotions, and behaviours by observing how they *relate* to one another. To understand a script, we need to know which lines belong to which characters. Likewise, to decode our inner words, we can begin by naming the voices that speak them.

The word "voice" is not perfect, but it makes a compelling metaphor for your inner patterns. The voices within us, like the people in our lives, may stick around for a day or a lifetime. They can learn and evolve. They can have a negative or positive impact on our confidence, mood, and livelihood from day to day. They can get along and help each other, or they can disagree and wage conflicts. And they can use those conflicts as opportunities to learn and grow.

This metaphor might not be new to you. You might imagine yourself as having an inner critic or a Higher Self. You might say that you hear your parents in your head. You might express inner conflict as "One part of me says to stay, and another says to go." We tend to understand things better when we give them human qualities. We do this to the gods we believe in as much as we do it to our patterns of emotion and reaction. We can use this tendency to facilitate self-understanding.

Your inner conversation is full of different voices. Notably, mental self-talk plays only a small part. You could call self-awareness a voice: your inner truth seeker. You could say your body has a voice. And your body is also a collection of other voices: your legs, stomach, head, spleen, skin, etc. Every voice is bound to be *part of* as well as *full of* other conversations. Some voices, such as the stomach, we all hear. Other voices are unique to each person. For example, some people self-communicate with auditory hallucinations. They literally hear voices. Still, we could sort the personalities of those voices into relatable categories: fear, self-doubt, judgment, anger. The *types* of voices we hear are similar, yet the way we experience them is unique to each of us. Thus, the way we label and interact with these patterns must be unique as well.

As we dive into this part of our metaphor, remember that naming your inner patterns is like naming star constellations. The labels do not represent some universal, unshakeable truth. They simply describe one way to organize the dynamics of reality so that we can explore them. This goes for the word "voices" too. The word has no value if it doesn't help you understand yourself better. Labelling our patterns can be mind-opening or mind-closing. It depends on whether our intent is to solidify a static illusion of knowledge or to engage in a curious adventure to unfolding truth.

For every self-communication, we assume its message and its source. We spoke earlier about misinterpreting signals of aloneness or tiredness as hunger. Some part of us says "eat." We think it's the stomach. But is it? If you've eaten recently, chances are that your stomach isn't telling you to eat. If you can eliminate this possibility, then you can search for other options. Which other voices could be communicating to you with hunger? You might look at some common suspects: loneliness, boredom, tiredness. Once you formulate a hypothesis about which voice it could be, you might try to translate the message better. Why would tiredness tell you to eat? Maybe eating makes you feel sleepy and motivates you to go to bed. How do you know if this is the correct translation? Of course, you must try it. If you feel a binge coming on, you can try taking a nap. If you doze off every time, then you have likely interpreted better. If not, you might try another possibility. You must experiment to understand better.

Another voice we often mistranslate is control. For many years, I said I needed love. I would grasp for it in desperation. Then, when the person I was grasping for would turn toward me, I would shut down. Irritation would burn my veins. As soon as I managed to pull someone close to me, I'd push him or her away. I said I wanted love, but no one (myself included) bothered to check for the meaning of this word in my inner dictionary. A pill addict tells her dealer she wants candy. I told the people around me I wanted love. But control was my drug of choice.

You might be wondering how you can tell similar-sounding patterns apart from one another. For example, many people discover an intuitive inner voice as well as a fearful one. Both sometimes say, "Don't do that." How can you ever know which voice is speaking? How can you know if you are cautioning yourself out of wisdom or anxiety? This is an understandable concern, but do not worry. Trust the process. With practice, you will see that telling apart your inner voices is no harder than telling apart your aunt and your mother. They are different people. They could look very much alike, yet you would still know the difference. Compare that to two similar-looking women whom you pass by on the street. Intimacy and interaction breed familiarity. The more you listen to your inner voices, the more you will understand them. Begin to observe your patterns, and you will learn.

Learning to self-communicate is like learning a new language. When you know only twenty words, you have a limited ability to express yourself and comprehend others. When you have a wider vocabulary, you can better hope to understand and be understood. As you develop a bigger glossary of possible interpretations, you will learn the subtle differences between your inner voices and their messages. Do not worry about not being able to tell the difference right away.

At this point, you might expect me to list all the inner voices that you should find. Many experts throughout time have invented creative labels for different patterns of the human experience. Think of them all: mind, body, and spirit; ego, id, and superego; fear and intuition; inner child and inner adult; ego and soul; and countless others. These might be helpful to you, or they might not. For some people, deciphering between ego and soul is life-changing. Why? Maybe these people spent a lifetime mistaking their anxious thoughts for truth or ignoring their creative impulses. For whatever reason, separating those two patterns helps some people understand themselves better. Some, not all. What's more, the labels might become harmful to the same people they once helped! A person who separates ego from soul might develop a resentful relationship toward what he calls ego. Thus, he will be unable to use this part of himself to its full potential. He will scorn a vital part of his experience. Only three years prior, the same labels might have saved him from suicide.

No one can tell you which patterns you need to differentiate in your experience or what you should call them. One person can come along and separate your experience into seven distinct parts. Another could break it up into twenty overlapping components. Someone else could label you as one horrible thing and suggest a pill to fix it. As we change perspective, we change perception. Since your inner patterns are not only unique to you but also ever-changing, your labels must be as well. There is no list. There are only examples.

The process of discovering our inner voices has so often been outside in. We learn some label. We try it on. This might be helpful sometimes, but it might also help to go in the other direction. You can go from the inside out. Observe your experience. If you feel some desire, some aversion, some emptiness, some anger, allow yourself to observe it. Then, when you begin to interpret your experience as a desire *for* something, an aversion *to* something, emptiness *because* of something, anger *with* someone, allow yourself to observe this too. Then, when you feel the drive to *do* something about these feelings, observe that as well. Each compulsion is an answer, but what is the question? As you continue to watch your inner conversation this way, you will begin to notice patterns. Then, you will notice patterns among those patterns. Like this, you can discover the characters in your inner drama as well as your power to lead them to peace.

Through intimate self-observation, you will become aware of the definitions you've scribed in your inner dictionary. Thus, you can find translation errors. You might think a daydream is literal, but it isn't. You might assume that some feeling is physical, but it's emotional. You might think something is part of your personality, but it's a symptom of lifelong misunderstanding. The more clearly you hear the messages of your inner voices, the more clearly they will speak to you. Their advice will start to match your actual needs. Voices that communicate by screaming will learn to whisper. Voices that sound alike will begin to sound different.

For example, as I was quitting smoking, I found thoughts that said, "I need a cigarette." I realized these thoughts were not true. No one *needs* a cigarette. Plenty of humans go without smoking, and a nicotine craving is not *that* powerful. So what did those thoughts mean? I discovered two distinct patterns that both communicated with cigarette cravings. First, I had these thoughts at routine times: when I woke up, when I got off the bus, after meals, and every hour. Considering that I had a history of addiction, I thought these were part of my "addictive personality." Second, I had cravings when I experienced overwhelming emotions—stress, anger, shame, gloom. I labelled these as my inner child.

As I explored my so-called addictive personality, I realized that it was a symptom, not a cause. My inner addict was a foot soldier for two voices that had taken over my inner conversation: anxiety and control. Through addictive impulses, these dictatorial patterns gave me shots of certainty to keep me calm. To address this, I worked hard to detach from my thoughts, decrease my stress levels, become more mindful, and develop purposeful routines that made me feel a sense of self-control. As my relationship with anxiety and control changed, my so-called addictive personality disappeared. With my inner child, it was a different story. If I craved a cigarette when I felt anger or sadness brewing, I knew I was in for the long haul. I would clear my schedule and make time to process my emotions. I would journal, hold myself, and cry. Then, I learned to reach out to other people. Because this part of me has received nourishing support so many times, it now communicates more clearly: with cravings for emotional release.

When we listen more consciously to our inner voices, the way they speak to us changes. This kind of transformation is possible in any relationship. Listening to others with an open, curious mind will help you understand them. And when they feel seen, most people act differently than when they feel judged.

From reading my story (especially if you smoke), you might find yourself scrambling to find your own addictive personality and inner child. And if you asked me how to quit smoking, I could say, "Decrease the anxiety fueling your addictive impulses and learn to manage your emotions better." This sounds like great advice. But what if you have a completely different relationship with smoking? What if cigarette cravings are messages from your low self-worth? What if you smoke as a way to self-destruct and sabotage yourself from moving forward in life? I've smoked for that reason at times, but it was not a pivotal cause for me. For someone else, however, this could be an important epiphany. No one knows which voices are important in your inner conversation except you.

For every voice you find, you can try to understand its habits. Each voice observes, interprets, and communicates about some part of reality. Let's say you notice that you often criticize yourself and label this part of you as "the inner critic." Which part of reality does it observe? Most people criticize themselves to some degree, but everyone judges different things. Some focus on their appearance. Some brood over their mistakes. Others pick apart their social skills. Then, you might explore how your inner critic interprets reality. How does this voice translate what it observes? Are its assumptions accurate? You can also notice how your inner critic speaks to you. This will help you understand how this pattern influences your life. For one person, the inner critic might perpetuate an alcohol addiction. For another, it could fuel academic achievement. The way we hear each voice depends on how it relates to the rest of our inner conversation: the relationships between our patterns, the way those patterns relate to the outside world, and the history of those relationships from birth to present. Nothing happens by itself. No answer comes from thin air.

Your inner voices are reflections of your past and present, your ideas and feelings, your hopes and fears. Each self-communication is a word spoken *by* you *to* you. You must interpret it according to your inner dictionary because you are speaking to yourself out of that same dictionary. For example, imagine that you begin daydreaming about selling all your possessions and moving to the mountains in India. What could it mean? Observe your experience. If you are working twelve-hour days at a job you loathe, and your spare time is filled with friends and family who don't understand you, then you might feel trapped. You might hypothesize that the daydream is your inner freedom-lover begging you to do things on your own terms more often. If you juggle your life around and, four months down the road, the daydream fades or disappears, you'll know you were right. However, if the dream persists, then maybe it has another message. Maybe it *is* literal. Or maybe it's your natural pace saying, "Don't rush, slow down." Or maybe it's your self-sabotage saying, "Don't rush, slow down" because you're close to a career breakthrough! The answers are not in any book. You must find them within yourself. Experiment. Run with your hunches, learn from the feedback, and keep a glass of doubt nearby.

The more you observe your patterns, the more you'll be able to separate your voices from the voices of other people. For example, you might feel blamed when talking to your friend. Your initial assumption might be that she is blaming you. But if you have become acquainted with the self-blaming voice in your head, you might catch yourself. *Is your friend blaming you, or is it that inner voice again, always interpreting other people's words as criticisms?* It could be either one or neither one. Self-awareness gives you the power to find out.

You can also begin to notice the difference between your real friend and your mental version of her. Each person in your life also exists as an inner voice. These mental characters can hold us back more than we realize—not only from fulfilling our potential but also from understanding the people they represent. For example, suppose that your father often criticized you as a child, so now you struggle with self-expression as an adult. Before you speak your truth to others, you rehearse in your head, and your mental father shuts you down. This hurts as much as if a real person were doing it. This process can go on for years after your father dies. But it can also go on for years after your father changes! Your mental father, instead of a dynamic representation, can become a static idea. Thus, you will not be able to see your real father beyond your ideas about him. Worse yet, this inner voice will influence your perception of comparable people. Older men with the same build who speak in a similar way. Older men with the same build. Older men. Men. Like this, we develop biases not only about the people in our lives but also about people we've never met. We typecast others into roles in our inner dramas. We rarely react to people as they are. Rather, we react to our mental versions of them. Self-awareness can help you discover and develop these inner voices. Even if your father is the same grumpy critic as he was all those years ago, you can try to understand him better. Why is he this way? What motivates his criticism? What keeps him from accepting others? Which qualities *do* you admire in him? Which of his negative qualities do you also see in yourself? Like this, you can find deep forgiveness.

By discovering other people's voices in your head, you can drive profound changes in your life. Maybe your father had a major role in your childhood. And let's suppose that he continues to have a major, not-so-helpful role in your life now. To change these dynamics in the outside world, you must first change them in your inner one. When you get on stage in front of your mental audience to play out possible future scenarios, for whom are you performing? Is your head full of people who criticize you and no one else? It's hard (if not impossible) to remove those people from your mind, but why do you need to? Once you've known someone, that person becomes an inner voice. You cannot help that. But it might be more helpful to put the critics in the back row and fill the rest of the theatre with people who support you. Then, you will not only receive the encouragement you desire, but you will also change your relationship with those critics. Once they no longer control you, you will be free to understand them, empathize with them, and even learn something from them (even if all you learn is a cautionary example!) Thus, you can change your relationship to your real father by changing how you relate to your mental version of him. By expanding your awareness, you will face the reality of that relationship. There, you will not find blame, judgment, or guilt. You will find ways to heal and grow without hurting or resenting him (or yourself).

Every human being is a multi-dimensional, ever-changing universe. To imagine someone as anything less is a disservice not only to that person but also to your search for truth. Thus, self-awareness can make you less judgmental. Once you discover the complex relationships between your inner voices, calling some of them "good" and others "bad" will seem nonsensical. And once you see this depth in yourself, how can you not see it in others? Your mental versions of people, instead of cardboard cutouts, will emulate conversations as deep and mysterious as your own.

Instead of searching for problems to fix, you can focus on healing individual voices and their relationships with one other. For example, imagine that you've been struggling with anxiety for some time and have spent thousands of dollars on unsuccessful cures. Instead of labelling yourself as broken, you might choose to look deeper: to become more aware of anxiety's role in your inner conversation. First, you might become aware of how anxiety speaks to you: tight chest, clenched throat, flushed face. Then, you might notice some thoughts that trigger it. Maybe it surfaces whenever you obsess over imperfections. You could define these obsessions as perfectionism. Diving deeper, you might find that perfectionism often observes your face and your choices, interprets them as flawed, and communicates to you in strong desires to fix your skin and your past. As you get to know perfectionism a bit more, you might notice this voice creeping up during social situations. Then, you might connect the dots between perfectionism and other symptoms you believed to be unrelated, such as pathological lying or awkwardness around new people. Imagine becoming aware of all this! None of those anxiety cures worked because anxiety was a symptom, not a cause. It was an important feedback mechanism about your perfectionist ideas.

So does this mean that perfectionism is the problem? If a problem is something to be labelled as "bad" and eradicated, then no, it isn't. Yes, perfectionism, in this case, is a cause rather than a symptom. But if you have a pattern of perfecting minor details, that pattern is not wrong. It just doesn't belong in a conversation about your face. Your face *is* imperfect, and so are your past choices. Trying to fix them is a losing battle. But not everything is like this. If you can steer your perfectionism toward some intricate skill that requires lifetime practice and refinement, you will experience a potent sense of self-mastery. You can also teach this voice to surrender its static notions and instead engage in a *process* of perfecting. Like this, the very pattern that once flared up your anxiety will begin to dance with creativity, self-confidence, and passion. There is magic in choosing curiosity over judgment.

Often, you will need to focus your healing efforts not on individual voices but on the relationships between them. For example, you might hear your inner adult dominating your inner child. Thus, your role will be to bring them to peace. Keep in mind that feuding voices are not always mental. For example, your stomach speaks to you through feelings of hunger, indigestion, and fullness. However, your relationship with it could deteriorate because of another voice—for example, shame. Shame could call you fat and tell you to stop eating. If you starved yourself enough, you would stop feeling hunger. Shame's mistranslations would warp the conversation between you and your digestive system. To fix this broken communication, you would first have to heal your relationship with shame. Yet even shame is not a useless hooligan that you need to exterminate. It can turn into a powerful ally. For example, shame can help us develop humility if we can learn to observe our shortcomings with curiosity and interpret them as opportunities for growth and acceptance.

In one of Aesop's fables, various body parts come together to talk about the troublesome stomach. They agree that the stomach is a useless waste of resources, so they decide to stop feeding it. Soon enough, the body housing all these parts begins to die, and they realize only too late that their scapegoat was a vital part of the unit. How many times in your life have you tried to "heal" by trying to destroy some apparently useless or harmful part of you? If you have failed at this, that's because it was doomed to fail. Healing is not divisive. All body parts matter. All the parts of you matter. Healing is not a matter of squelching some inner voices while enthralling others. Healing is a process of wholeness. It is a process of unity.

No pattern is always useless. A voice that was harmful ten minutes ago could be helpful in the present moment, and the voices that once kept you safe may one day keep you prisoner. Just like learning Spanish will not help you understand Swahili, so learning mistrust will not help you be intimate in relationships. There is a time and a place for Spanish, and there is a time and a place for mistrust. Nothing is a useless cyst for you to cut out of your experience, and nothing is a knight in shining armour—not even self-awareness. Everything relates, and everything matters.

Our culture says that to get rid of some ineffective habit, you must replace it with another. To quit smoking, use an e-cigarette. To stop self-judgment, think positive thoughts. To lose weight, eat kale. But if you don't understand the core needs that fuel your self-harming behaviours, you'll keep relapsing into them—no matter how healthy the replacements. If you do not understand your hunger, you cannot feed it. Observing your patterns will teach you self-compassion. You are not a broken object to be fixed. You are a complex puzzle to be unriddled. Once you experience this, you will never again reduce yourself to a static idea—no matter how attractive the marketing.

If you've been seeking solutions that end up harming you—looking for quick fixes from wise oracles—this is not random. A piece of advice might be useful or useless today, but deciphering usefulness is a pattern in itself. Just like there were voices within me that wanted power but spoke of violence, there might be voices within you that want solutions but speak of quick fixes. To heal your toxic relation-

ships with such voices, you must first observe how they relate to the context, to each other, and to you. Each voice is a
clue to your inner mystery. And still, each voice is a tool for
self-communication, a story about a pattern, a figment of
your imagination.

We have learned to ask, "What else is there?" We can
expand this question to ask, "Which other voices are there?"
We have learned to ask, "What am I observing? How am I
translating it? Is my translation accurate?" We can apply this
line of questioning to different parts of the inner conversation. We can focus on a specific self-communication and ask,
"What am I experiencing right now? Which voice do I believe
is speaking this way? Which other voices sound similar?" We
can also focus on a specific voice and ask, "What is *it* observing? How is it translating reality? Is that translation accurate?" And if it *is* likely accurate, we can ask, "Where else in
my inner conversation might this voice belong? Would it be
more helpful if it observed something else?"

Untangling your patterns of misinterpretation might
be difficult. Like a cat left in a room with balls of yarn, you
have twisted yourself into a mishmash. This was never your
fault, but now, it is your responsibility to untangle this
multicoloured mess. It's a big, frustrating job. As you try to
unwind one string, it drags dozens of others along with it.
But bit by bit, piece by piece, you will make progress. You
will unravel. You will heal.

A World Beyond Ideas

Have you ever lost something and, in the process of trying to
find it, looked in the same place more than once? Think of
how illogical this is. If your keys weren't in the couch the first
time, they won't be there the second time. And definitely

not the fifth time. But we check anyway. Why? Because they were there the last time we lost them. Or because that's where we usually lose them. Or because we can't think of where else to look. This behaviour is irrational and border-line neurotic, but we do it anyway. Maybe you react differently to losing your keys, but to some degree, we all do this: we get stuck on our ideas. To understand your self-communications better, you must question your assumptions. To know yourself, you must sacrifice the illusion that you already do.

It can be challenging to let go of our ideas about ourselves, about other people, about the past. I remember being on a bus one time when I was feeling particularly paranoid. I felt everyone's eyes on me. This was shortly after I began questioning my thoughts. So I decided to look up and check if people were indeed watching me. Of course, they weren't. But the moment I cast my eyes back down, my thoughts again screeched that people were watching. I looked back up. No one paid me any mind. Soon enough, I invented an even more paranoid theory: everyone on the bus was conspiring to look away whenever I looked up. To the voice of paranoia, this was the only reasonable conclusion. It took months of making these kinds of observations for me to return to social reality. But return I did. I allowed life's conversation to heal my inner one.

Why do we become so addicted to ideas that harm us? Why was I hooked on this notion that I was being watched when it was not only untrue but also harmful to my well-being?

We can compare our attachment to ideas to another common addiction: food. We all need to eat. However, some people use food to fuel their bodies, whereas others use it for emotional regulation. Food addiction is not about food. It's about loneliness, sadness, boredom, or whatever voice speaks with food cravings. Interpretation is the same. We must formulate ideas about the world to live within it. Yet some of us use ideas for understanding, while others use ideas for comfort. Stubbornness is not about the concepts we defend. It's about shame, self-worth, fear, or whatever voice convinces us that being right will make everything okay. The cause of these addictions is the same: mistranslation. Yet the journey to healing is also the same: awareness. By observing our emotions and bodies, we can heal our relationships with food. Likewise, by observing uninterpreted reality, we can begin to heal our inner voices.

"Uninterpreted" is not a word. Although the spell checker's squiggly, red line is a punishing stimulus, I insist on keeping this word. If we cannot recognize the existence of a reality beyond our ideas, then we have no way to check for mistranslations. To understand better, we must return to observation. We must ask questions about the world around us instead of hoarding answers. And the first, most important question is this: "What if I have no idea what's going on?"

Uninterpretation is the art of playing with ideas—knocking them over like a house of cards before we begin building again. Of course, we cannot erase ideas. We can knock over a house of cards, but we cannot delete our memory of building one. Even the most curious child remembers what she learned yesterday. Even the most open-minded observer still interprets the difference between a wall and an empty space when he is walking down the street. Uninterpretation is not a process of losing all our ideas. That is impossible. Rather, it is a conscious recognition of a world beyond those ideas: a truth that dwarfs all our interpretations of it. Life's mysterious conversation.

When people say things like "life is meaningless," they are rarely smiling. Such thoughts can perpetuate depression or even lead to suicide. After all, if life has no meaning, then what is the point? But what if these people have simply become aware of the pane of glass between themselves and the world? What if they've begun to contemplate the existence of a reality beyond their conceptions of it? What if they've begun the journey of self-awareness but stopped short because the outside world taught them to label this experience as "bad"?

Meaning is something we ascribe to things in order to understand them. Reality itself is meaningless. Once this jagged, little pill digests within us, it unlocks a beautiful gift: free will. If we can change how we perceive the world, we can make choices. We can heal. We can forge a different path than the one of least resistance. Most importantly of all, we can seek what is true beyond what we already think we know.

Observing uninterpreted reality can help us detach from our assumptions. In grade school, for example, we would recite a word like "egg" until it sounded strange and foreign. Egg. Egg. Egg. Thus, "egg" would become an observable sound rather than a symbol for the tangible object it represented. By experiencing the word in its raw, uninterpreted form, we would momentarily free it from the meaning we'd learned to give to it. We neither forgot our existing definition nor replaced it. We simply invited a new perspective.

Uninterpretation allows us to align our inner conversation to reality. We can put our ideas on tracing paper and match them to our observations and experiences. Too often, it's the other way around. We try to squeeze the present moment into our preconceived notions. Then, we get frustrated when it doesn't fit. Uninterpretation is an act of deep humility. We surrender control, bow our heads, and ask life to show us the way. We calibrate our inner world to our outer one. This takes an immense amount of trust, yet it also reaps unmatched rewards.

Observing reality can help us dethrone our mental dictators. With some voices, it is difficult to separate their abusive insults and destructive advice from the truth. Then, when other people parrot our judgmental self-talk, we ruminate on what they've said. The words that hurt us the most are the ones we take personally. But how can anything be personal? If someone gives you advice, she is telling you what *she* believes. If someone calls you a name, he is showing you how *he* thinks. What people say is a reflection of how *they* interpret the world. It is the same with the voices within us. How they speak to us does not reflect who we are. It only reflects how those voices observe, interpret, and react to reality. Those reactions might be useful or harmful. They might originate in understanding or misunderstanding. By taking *all* your voices with a grain of salt, you can liberate yourself from self-abuse.

Some years ago, I decided to work on accepting my makeup-free, natural face. Every time I looked at myself in the mirror, the same old self-loathing voice would pipe up. It would tell me about how ugly, fat, and revolting I was. I observed this voice, and I also observed the face it was talking about. I looked at the shapes, colours, and lines. I saw it as meaningless visual information. I saw my uninterpreted face while listening to my interpretations about it. In those moments, I experienced myself. I *felt* who I was. Thus, I realized I couldn't reduce myself to *any* idea. This weakened the power that my self-critical thoughts had over me. And once I was no longer the victim of my inner voices, I could work on understanding them.

Again and again, I have said, "Let experience teach you." Now, we can expand this sentence: let your experience of uninterpreted reality teach you how to interpret it. Yes, it is a big paradox: recognizing that all ideas are imperfect can help you perfect your ideas. They say, "If you love something, let it go; if it comes back, then it is yours." Ideas are the same way. The truth endures.

The same goes for this book. If you apply these words to your life, then you can experience and evaluate them. If you do not apply them, they remain ideas. You may think I've invented them and like me better for it. Or you might suspect that I stole them and call me unethical for it. Neither attitude will help you understand yourself better. The ideas will not help. The ideas herein are unoriginal simply because they reflect the human experience. Anything true can be experienced by anyone, anywhere. What I am sharing with you here has been written and said thousands of times throughout history by just as many people. When fresh eyes see the same view, maybe that view has some merit. This applies to your inner world too. Look without judgment, and the validity of your judgments will become clear.

Again, uninterpreting reality does not require you to force ideas out of your head. We cannot erase existing interpretations. We cannot go backward. We can only go forward. This is what I mean by uninterpretation: moving forward by moving back. Continuing by returning. This is not as absurd as it seems. A blade of grass sticks straight up. When the wind comes, it bends. The stronger the wind, the more it bends. When the wind eases, however, the blade straightens. It continues by returning, goes forward by coming back. Like this, you can allow your mind to fill with ideas, and then allow it to empty of them.

You do not need to fight interpretation just like you do not need to fight the wind. You cannot fight the wind. You cannot fight interpretation. You are an intelligent being. Of course you will try to formulate ideas about what you observe. Of course you will invite the people you respect and fear to reside as voices in your head. You are human. This is normal. It happens to everyone. Uninterpretation is simply a choice you make after you take on a solid idea—a choice to look beyond, to question, to observe.

Curiously, you will find that there is no need to force this part of self-awareness. There is no need to induce emptiness upon yourself when you are full. When you've had enough food, your body gives you signals to stop eating so that digestion can lead you back to emptiness. You do not need to control this process. It functions well. You simply need to allow what is already happening to happen. As you watch yourself nearing fullness, you can observe a desire to return to emptiness. This goes for being full on food as much as social contact, sensory stimulation, and physical activity. Think of a wave: it washes onto the shore, and then it rolls back. Likewise, each of your activities has a backside of stillness. To be with people, you must be alone. To listen, you need silence. To exercise, you need rest. You do not need to inflict rest, silence, or aloneness. You can simply surrender to your existing urges for these essential actions. This is how it works with interpretation as well. As you fill your mind with ideas, an urge will arise to release them. If you don't have such urges, you are probably mistranslating them.

Perhaps you have misread your desire for uninterpretation as depression or even the urge to self-harm. Perhaps you have translated it as a craving for alcohol or television. It is possible that each time you have felt yourself rolling back into the mystery of the present moment, you have reached for food, sleep, drugs, drink—whatever you thought would fix it. When we feel a hole widening within us, we scramble to fill it. We work so hard to avoid feeling empty, but emptiness is essential. Allow that hole to widen. Let it eat you alive. The void is as important as the fullness.

Here is an even more fascinating possibility: your cravings for ultimate right answers might be mistranslated cravings for uninterpretation. Your desire for certainty might actually be a desire to let go of it. How can this be? It is not as bizarre as it sounds. You interpret the world to understand it, to seek truth. But truth is more than just ideas. A truth seeker needs to conceptualize reality *and* observe it. So the voice of self-awareness has two messages. Sometimes, it leads you toward an idea. Other times, it leads you toward reality. You might interpret these nudges as the same feeling.

This kind of confusion—where we lump two opposing desires into one—is not as uncommon as you might think. For years, I struggled with overeating. When I felt full, my stomach would send me signals of discomfort. Obviously, these meant "Stop eating!" But food helped me deal with my emotions, including discomfort. So I would try to eat away the discomfort of overeating! I found a similar misunderstanding when I learned the importance of rest and solitude. I interpreted feelings of irritation as signals to work harder when, sometimes, they were urging me to step away. I interpreted my annoyance with people to mean that I needed their attention when, sometimes, it meant that I needed to be alone. When we have just one definition for two words, we can only understand so much.

Once you stop resisting your urge to uninterpret, you might start to translate this simple desire as a craving for a specific technique. Some people find benefits in meditation, energy work, or therapy. Others loosen their thoughts by movement. They run, sing, dance. Some let go of ideas by externalizing them. They journal, paint, talk. Sometimes, simple things do the trick: crying, going on a nature walk, or even just sitting quietly. But no method is immune to the winds of change. If you ate the same dinner daily, you'd tire of it—no matter how much you love that dish today. Likewise, all tactics and techniques grow old. Allow this. Plan for this. Listen to the simplest version of each self-communication. Thus, you can remain aware of your basic needs while allowing your methods of fulfilling those needs to change. The foods you eat will vary over time, but your need for food will remain constant. The beds you sleep in, whom you sleep in them with, and how long you sleep for will change, yet your need for sleep will not. So experiment with various methods of uninterpretation, but keep in mind that you need it. If you do not like my made-up word, use your own. It is not the word that matters but your awareness of this pattern in your experience. Don't just believe me when I say it. Look for yourself.

Releasing old ideas is often a slow process. No matter how painful our relationships with certain voices, we get used to them. There is no timeline and no final goal. Focus on opening your doors each time they close, and that will be enough. Over time, it will get easier. The more you entertain new ideas, the easier it will become for you to detach from them. The process will take on a more natural pace, like the flow of breath in and out of your body. You will let go of ideas as effortlessly as you exhale.

Once you fall into a steady ebb and flow of interpretation, you might experience a curious side effect: an influx of imagination. This might seem counterintuitive. After all, imagination is a willful detachment from reality. Yet there is a difference between being stuck in our interpretation patterns and curiously exploring different perspectives. Instead of being addicted to our daydreams and worries, we can allow ourselves to play with how we see the world. We can twist reality into unexpected shapes and sort it into interesting boxes. We can build something beautiful, and we can just as easily tear it down. Like this, creativity thrives. As does inspiration. This may sound familiar. As a child, you played with your interpretations. Thus, some people might consider this a childish regression, a wasteful setback, a step backward. It isn't. It is remarkable progress. To access a child mind as an adult is no easy feat. It takes work. A child does not decide to be open-minded. As a self-aware adult, you make conscious choices. You earn back your right to be free, to play, to exist without struggling. And that is an accomplishment worth celebrating.

Looking At Yourself

The degree to which a person can grow is directly proportional to the amount of truth he can accept about himself without running away.

LELAND VAL VAN DE WALL

✖ ✖ ✖ ✖ ✖ ✖ ✖ ✖

Remember a time when you heard your voice on a recording or saw yourself on video. Better yet, think of when this happened to you by surprise. How did you react? Were you intrigued, excited, grateful? Or did you grimace, hold your breath, and hope that it would end quickly? Do you take every opportunity to hear and see yourself (as you would with someone you care about)?

Most of us would rather not. The way we approach ourselves is the polar opposite of how we approach those we love. With eager, sparkling eyes, we observe the people we cherish. With fearful, pained expressions, we avoid the image and sound of ourselves. Curiously, this is not limited to people with abusive, self-judging voices in their heads. And it isn't limited to our physical selves either. Looking at our behaviours, emotions, and thoughts in a candid way can be just as uncomfortable.

In addition to your mental versions of others, you also have a mental version of yourself. You have a certain understanding of what you look like, what you sound like, what other people think of you, what you excel at, etc. This is the most pervasive character in your inner drama. It influences how you define, understand, and relate to the world around you. If you have a static self-concept, you will put static labels onto other people. If you allow for a dynamic self-concept, you will allow and expect changes in others. If you believe, without a doubt, that you know who you are, you will be just as certain about your judgments of others. The more you distort yourself, the more you will distort the world. Now here is something interesting: you already distort yourself more than anything or anyone else.

The recorded voice sounds strange to you, but how do you know what you sound like? You're the only one who hears the particular way your voice resonates as it vibrates through your ear canals. Other people do not gasp in horror at your recording because they recognize it. To them, this is how you've sounded all along. The recorded voice is not the anomaly. Your experience of it is.

When you see yourself in photographs or videos, that person does not match whom you see in the mirror. First, your reflection is reversed, so the photos and videos seem backward. Second, you are accustomed to seeing your body from a certain distance and angle. Seeing yourself from 4 feet away or looking up at yourself from 4 feet below is not common. Thus, these points of view can be distressing. However, a co-worker whose desk is 4 feet away from yours or a child who is 4 feet shorter sees you from that viewpoint all the time. Finally, in posture and facial expression, you might be accustomed to your "mirror look," which doesn't reflect most of your emotional spectrum. Even if you smile at yourself in the mirror, this is not the same smile that others see when they amuse or compliment you. The expressions and gestures of the person in the photograph or video may look foreign to you, but you are the only one who feels this way. The people around you know exactly that person. They do not know the person in the mirror.

In addition to static ideas, this is another potential obstacle: static perspectives. You look different from day to day. You watch yourself getting older. You know this. Modern-day marketing, if anything, has helped you focus on this *more*. The mirror might show a dynamic image, but you see it from a static viewpoint.

Imagine a world without mirrors. Other people would see us a certain way, and we would experience ourselves a different way. We could only imagine how we look to others. We believe that the mirror branches this gap, but this is an illusion. The mirror provides us with only one way of looking at ourselves. There are countless other perspectives.

We face similar obstacles with observing our thoughts, emotions, and behaviours. We are used to the distortions offered by our self-concepts. We are used to seeing ourselves as having certain personality traits, abilities, and desires. We are used to justifying our actions and others' reactions in familiar ways. We are accustomed to our self-preservation instincts. Curiously, no one else knows who we think we are. No one else knows your mental version of yourself. Other people only know *their* mental versions of you. We tend to assume that others see us as we see ourselves, and these assumptions further strengthen our self-concepts. The more detached our ideas about ourselves are from the truth, the more difficult self-observation becomes.

Looking at ourselves honestly can be overwhelming. Observing other people's unedited reactions to us can be humiliating. But ignorance comes with its own price, whether or not we acknowledge paying it. Discomfort is crucial to self-observation. Our inner mirrors, like our inner windows, can be dirty or clean. Every ounce of truth you drink from the present moment washes away your assumptions. Awareness strips you naked. It hurts, but it also heals.

We all experience different levels of unease when we start observing ourselves. This depends on how much of a chasm there is between how we are and how we think we are. A self-aware person might feel uncomfortable watching herself on videotape, but not for long. She will soon embrace this new viewpoint and maybe even commit to exploring it more often. Few of us have it so easy! From there, we can add multiple levels of interpretation that make self-observation more difficult. Your self-concept can cause you to warp your reflection. You can develop distorted ideas about what you look like to the point that you can't recognize yourself in photos or videos.

Those who have thick dust on their inner mirrors have much more work to do. Some people only need to overcome the mild discomfort of shifting perspectives, while others must first face their abusive inner voices. Some people hyperfocus on their flaws and mistakes. For them, it is difficult to see their potential beyond their self-criticism. Others hide behind grandiose adjectives and egotism. For them, it is just as difficult to see their messy, imperfect selves beneath their narcissism. For many of us, facing the truth about ourselves is not easy. And for some of us, it is the hardest thing we will ever learn to do. Some of us must break through not only our layers of distorted interpretations but also the multi-generational cycles that have passed those patterns on to us. It isn't easy. But it is worthwhile. For our healing and for the health of our society, this is the most important work there is. And it begins with curiosity—with wonder about who we are.

I had the strange experience, in my teenage years, of accidentally observing my reflection, not knowing it was me. In my head, I was fat and ugly. The girl in the mirror was beautiful. I hadn't yet interpreted that girl through my self-image. I felt deep envy for this person who I thought was so much more beautiful than I was. My ideas about myself envied my actual self! This was a bizarre experience, but the strangest thing of all was that I did not learn from it. At least, not back then. Within a few months, I actually forgot that it had happened! Retrospectively, this seems as ludicrous as forgetting that your house is on fire, but I had ironclad ideas about myself that I didn't realize I could question. The incident did not fit with my narrative about what was going on, so I forgot it. Many years and several epiphanies later, a memory of this episode returned—ripe with lessons.

My first step, as I already shared, was to look at my reflection through two lenses: the eyes of self-loathing and the eyes of self-awareness. This was the beginning of a much longer journey. I realized, for example, that I had an unhealthy relationship with the scale. I used it to measure my worth, and I only stepped on it when I felt fat. I also had a tendency to use full-length mirrors only to criticize my body. At first, I tried to hide from these perspectives. I threw out my scale and put my mirror under the bed. This eased my anxiety but did not eliminate it. The world is full of scales and full-length mirrors. (Sometimes in surprising places!) Instead of using them as tools to feed my self-loathing, I realized I could change my relationship with them.

I started weighing myself at different times—not only when I felt bloated. In the morning, in the evening. Before a meal, after a meal. Different parts of my menstrual cycle. I found something fascinating: the numbers meant nothing! They changed constantly and didn't reflect how I felt at all. In reality, my weight only represented the relationship between my body and Earth's gravity. On Mars or the moon, the number would be different. I realized that placing my self-confidence in the hands of the scale was as ludicrous as placing my mood in the hands of the weather. It was a recipe for helplessness.

I also started making eye contact with myself in the mirror instead of looking only at my so-called flaws. I began to drink in my entire reflection. My body, under a loving gaze, became an organic life form full of blood, muscles, and energy. Instead of seeing my thighs as objects to evaluate, I saw them as strong vehicles that transported me from place to place. I started to enjoy exercise more than ever. Now, instead of trying to look a certain way, I work on maintaining the health of this precious vessel. To love and nurture it like a mother does a child.

When we spend a lifetime focusing on some part of us that triggers negative self-talk, it feels like the answer is to stop looking at ourselves from that perspective. But we are intelligent beings. Our eyes refuse to unsee what they've seen. To avoid something that we know exists feels like brainwashing, forced ignorance. We resist.

Imagine trying to avoid or ignore an addictive craving. You can only distract yourself for so long. Worse yet, the more you push it away, the stronger it pushes back. You might hold off for a while longer, but when you indulge, you'll want more. Now imagine approaching the same situation with self-awareness. You can see the addictive thoughts and observe which voice you think is speaking. You can ponder other possibilities. Then, you can try to shift perspectives. Instead of focusing only on the momentary feeling, you can look into the past and future. You can remember the regret and shame you have felt after indulging this craving, and you can anticipate how you will feel if you give in to it now. You can remember other addictions you've conquered and how it feels to master your behaviours. You might imagine all the resources and emotions that will become available to you without this addiction. You might think of a friend who quit and remember her advice. You might look at yourself through the eyes of a child or another person who treasures you and would never hurt you. There are countless perspectives that can help you see more of the situation. By playing with your ideas and viewpoints, you will not be able to seduce yourself. You will not be blind to the consequences of your actions or the origins of your desires. Thus, you can make the choices that are best for you rather than the ones that are most familiar.

Playing with perspectives is particularly interesting when it comes to looking through other people's eyes. We tend to put our thoughts into others' heads. This can be devastating. When we cast other people as critics and villains in our inner dramas, this perpetuates our self-abuse *and* sabotages our intimate relationships.

Notice your assumptions about how others see you, what they think of you, what they want from you. Do your stories about other people's perceptions mimic your self-concept? Catch yourself. Have a laugh about it. Try again. What else could they be thinking, feeling, desiring? Open yourself to the full spectrum of human experience. Wonder. What if you've never seen yourself as they see you?

Breaking through these distortions can be difficult and shame-inducing. If everything you've assumed about other people's perceptions is inaccurate, wouldn't this mean that you've been wasting your time? When we emerge from a lifetime underground, sunshine is bittersweet. But our years of blindness can teach us important lessons—ones that are difficult to learn any other way. From casting others as characters in your inner drama, you can see them doing the same to you. How other people perceive you reflects their level of self-awareness. If they live with dirty windows and mirrors, they will see you as darkly as they see themselves. If they make a daily effort to seek truth and question their assumptions, they will treat you with the same respect.

Look at yourself through others' eyes. Take every perspective. What looks like a flaw to one person looks like radiant beauty to another. What is embarrassing to one is authentic to the next. What is funny to some is offensive to others. For everything you want to fix about yourself, there is someone who will accept it. And for everything you love about yourself, there is someone who would want you to change it. Look from every angle.

You might be concerned about taking perspectives that showcase you in a negative light. Especially if you've struggled with self-esteem, it might seem counterproductive to look at yourself through the eyes of a person who hates you. But a perspective is not a static thing. It is a relationship. Looking at yourself through the eyes of a hateful person can help you understand that person. It can help you understand hate, hunger, and human suffering. Once you embrace the bigger picture—how all different kinds of people can view you, react to you, and relate to you—you will not be able to take *anyone's* actions or opinions too personally. Once you realize how closely people's judgments echo their narratives, you will stop working so hard to influence their perceptions of you. Best of all, you will learn to question your inner voices. Abuse needs silence and isolation, including self-abuse. The more you invite various perspectives into your head, the more you will undermine the authority of your mental dictators. Even if those viewpoints are not "positive," they're still real; and even bittersweet reality will heal the wounds of misunderstanding.

Intention is key. Some people use the word "self-consciousness" as a synonym for what I call self-awareness. Yet others use it to mean a more unpleasant experience: a nervous preoccupation with how we appear to others. In yoga and meditation, students learn to become aware of their breathing. Yet in grade school, kids would say, "You are now aware of your breathing" as a cruel joke. How awareness affects us depends on our objective. If we try to look at ourselves with the intention to understand, then no matter what we find, we succeed. Even if we find something unpleasant, we can be glad because at least we've become conscious of it. On the other hand, when we observe ourselves only to feed our ideas about who we are, we can find the same things and use them to justify our distorted narratives.

It all comes back to curiosity. We live in a society that objectifies us as sexual objects and status symbols. We learn to flatten ourselves and others into little words: good and bad, ugly and pretty, right and wrong, lovable and unlovable. Then, we try to discover who we are through these labels. It doesn't work. Because a human being is more than a signpost onto which we can plaster our judgments. A person is more than a sack of flesh to lose, keep, or throw away. A human being cannot be packaged into a stale idea. A person must be experienced to be known, and this knowledge ends the moment you stop looking. Each one of us is a mystery. And the more aware you become, the more mysterious it gets. The reward for seeking truth is not the truth itself. The gift is wonder. The gift is love.

The Great Balancing Act

Your hand opens and closes, opens and closes. If it were always a fist or always stretched open, you would be paralysed. Your deepest presence is in every small contracting and expanding, the two as beautifully balanced and coordinated as birds' wings.

RUMI

Have you ever been in an argument where the other person turned frantic while you remained calm without much effort? It is tempting, in such situations, to invent stories like "I kept my composure because an intense reaction was unnecessary." These kinds of explanations make us feel good about ourselves. They give us the impression that we are making choices about our behaviours. But while these interpretations might serve our egos, they do little for our relationships and even less for our pursuit of truth.

As the calm person, you might feel tempted to place all sorts of unkind labels upon the person in front of you: hysterical, crazy, manipulative. But remember, if you can, a time when the tables were turned. Have *you* ever been the one raising your voice and bursting with emotion while your argument partner stood stone cold? From this perspective,

122

your experience is different. As the emotional person, you might say, "I am upset about what you did, and now you're ignoring how I feel, which only makes me feel worse!" You might label that person as cold, withholding, cruel.

All along, we believe we're making choices. We say, "I chose not to react." We say, "I chose not to shut down." Then, we blame the people in front of us because they're not making the same choices as we are. We say, "I am not getting angry at you, so why are you getting angry at me?" We say, "I am not ignoring you, so why are you ignoring me?" These kinds of dynamics destroy relationships. Yet these patterns are symptoms of something larger. External conflict originates within.

Every person has the capacity to be emotional as well as apathetic. We can feel, and we can stop feeling. We can care, and we can stop caring. It might be tempting to say that one is better than the other, but each has its place. When a friend is going through a hard time, our emotions can fuel empathy and connection. Yet our feelings can also trap us in abusive and dangerous circumstances. When our children and partners need to express their emotions, apathy can keep us from listening and bonding. Yet detachment can also help us overcome people pleasing and address injustice. Every voice has its place.

Even when one voice seems more useful, its opposite is always a valuable part of the conversation. Yes, you need emotions to connect to your friend, but if you become *too* attached to her problems, you might wear yourself thin and prevent her from learning her own lessons. Yes, you need apathy to walk away from abusive situations, but without some compassion for yourself as well as your abuser, you will cultivate resentment. Yes, you need emotions to help you listen to your loved ones, but what if they are upset with you? When we're triggered, we tend to exaggerate, to hyperfocus, to say "always" and "never." If you take those words at face value, you might jeopardize not only your peace of mind but also your relationship with that person. Ironically, a healthy level of detachment is crucial to empathetic listening. And while apathy can help us become more assertive and ask for what we need, without some sensitivity, we can unnecessarily hurt people. Just because some things need to be said doesn't mean we can't say them in a kind way. We need emotions *and* apathy in our inner conversations. Both have something valuable to contribute.

As the calm person in an argument, you spotlight apathy. You detach from your emotions as well as the emotional experience of the other person. As the reactive person, you fixate on emotions. You feel your distress, *and* you feel the other person's callousness. This is what keeps the argument going. Yet neither person is wholly wrong. Each is only doing half the job. As the apathetic person, you succeed in not taking things personally. This is integral to effective communication. As the emotional person, you remain open and sensitive to your feelings as well as the other person's. This is just as important. The argument persists because each person is playing only one role in a bigger conversation— taking one perspective on a truth that encompasses both.

The emotional person's job, then, is to invite a bit of apathy. To say, "Your stonewalling isn't personal. I don't need to take your disgust and distance so close to heart. This is your unconscious reaction. It is not a reflection of my worth." And the aloof person's job is to invite some feeling. To say, "Your outburst is happening for a reason. You feel something, and this is how you're expressing it. Your feelings are valid, and I am sure I would feel the same in your shoes." Like this, the argument can end. Of course, even after the emotional person calms down, he might still feel triggered by whatever sparked the fight. And the apathetic person might reach out, but she might still feel manipulated by the intensity of her partner's reaction. There is so much more to do! But after they've both embraced each other's perspectives, they can begin to tackle their issues at the root. They can communicate about the situation and achieve a common understanding. They can problem-solve instead of just arguing.

A crucial step in overcoming these kinds of conflicts is accepting how unconscious these patterns are. If someone angers you and you make an effort to calm down before you respond, you can say you're making a choice. However, when someone screams at you and you suddenly go numb, this is not a choice. This is a self-protective impulse. Likewise, if someone hurts you and, despite your initial defensiveness, you make an effort to reach out and provide some comfort, that's a choice. However, when someone pulls away from you and you desperately chase after that person, trying to get a reaction, this is not a choice. It is an automatic response. Without thinking, we counterbalance other people's reactions. We cannot eliminate these reflexes just like we cannot avoid a stretched rubber band snapping back into place. However, if we learn to observe these patterns, they do not have to control us. We can take every urge to counterbalance another person as a signal of imbalance between some of our inner voices.

If you prevented yourself from breathing in, this would be just as harmful as preventing yourself from breathing out. The inhalation and exhalation of air is a balanced process, a perfect cycle. There are such cycles between your inner voices. We have already explored the balance between taking on ideas and releasing them. There are infinite others. Everything has a backside. In these pages, we will use the words "balance" and "imbalance" to describe these relationships. When you invite all paradoxes into your inner chambers, we will call this inner balance. When you shun or idealize some voices, we will call this imbalance.

Life's conversation is already balanced, but your inner conversation might not be. What does it mean that life's conversation is balanced? It means, simply, that contradictory patterns exist within the structure of reality. Of course, they do not always exist at even ratios. (There aren't precisely 3.8 billion extroverts to every 3.8 billion introverts!) While "balance" sometimes describes equal proportions, this is not what I mean by this word. Here, balance refers to the coexistence of counteracting forces: opposing actions, ideas, and perspectives. Reality is a house of paradoxes. So is a truth seeker's mind.

Likely, you have identified your self-communications about imbalance as problems. Addiction to drugs and people, perfectionism, codependency, impulse control problems, resentment, blame, difficulty forgiving, envy, toxic relationships—these can all be symptoms of imbalance. In seeking the roots of these phenomena, you might discover that much of your suffering has a common cause.

Balance is an important director of our thoughts, feelings, and desires. Too often, we think of balance as something we must *do*, otherwise it remains undone. Yet while we can take actions to balance our inner conversations, balance is more than an action we take. It is a dimension of reality. It is a stitch pattern in the fabric of life. It is a property of the ever-flowing, ever-changing conversation between all things. Our task is not to impose balance upon an imbalanced system. Balance is already happening. What we *can* do is notice what balance is *already* doing. Thus, you can begin to see your most troublesome patterns through a new lens.

If you keep ending up in toxic relationships or having the same problems in different jobs, you can stop blaming yourself. *And* you can stop blaming your partners, bosses, and friends. By discovering balance—the invisible puppeteer—you can see how it pulls your heartstrings. Then, you can make different choices.

The Hero and the Villain

During my brief stint in theatre school, I learned about a trick that playwrights use called "foils." A foil is a contrasting character. For example, if the protagonist of a story is humble, brave, and compassionate, her foil would be egotistical, cowardly, and selfish. The interactions between these two characters would highlight their prevailing traits. The word "foil" comes from the 16th-century practice of putting metal foil as a backing on gems to make them shinier. The villain exists to shine a light on the qualities of the hero, and vice versa.

The most interesting thing about foils is that, without them, stories are bland. "Once upon a time, there was a man who was very good, did good things, and ended up very happy. The end." No one wants to hear this story. We want conflict, clashes, obstacles. We do not simply want goodness to exist. We want to see it triumph over evil. We want a compelling narrative.

The hero defines the villain, and the villain defines the hero, yet neither is real. How many pure heroes do you know who are nothing but brave, humble, and strong? How many pure villains do you know who are nothing but menacing, manipulative, and evil just for evil's sake? Eventually, every hero topples off his pedestal and turns out to have flaws, like anyone else. And every villain's iron facade cracks open to reveal insecurities, weaknesses, and all too often, a sad story. Pure good and pure evil exist in meta-

127

phors, stories, and delusions rather than everyday experiences. Still, many popular books, movies, and plays continue to stage the hero-villain drama. Why? Why are we so captivated by characters that do not represent our experiences with real human beings?

We could say that we feel drawn to illusions of perfection and wish to see ourselves in the heroes we admire. But if you were to read a whole book about good people without any flaws or obstacles, you would soon grow bored (or ashamed, depending on how you interpreted it). You can hate and loathe the villain, but without her, the hero would be intolerable. Perhaps, then, something is happening outside our conscious awareness. Perhaps it is not the individual characters we are so fond of but the conversation between them—a conversation that is ongoing within us.

The image of a devil on one shoulder and an angel on the other has appeared so often in our visual and written arts that it has become a cliché. Symbols of good and evil are common for the same reason that words like "cloud" and "hair" exist in every language around the world: the more common the experience, the more common the symbols.

We label some parts of ourselves as "good" and others as "bad." We want the good to replace the bad, to conquer it. But this never actually happens, does it? Just when we think we are rid of some pesky, useless inner voice, it returns—sometimes louder than before! Just as we begin to celebrate our mastery of some skill or understanding, we falter. The victory of good over evil is, at best, temporary.

Sometimes, we search outside ourselves for villains and saviours. These triumphs are just as fleeting. Every time we think we have been saved by some hero—whether that is a person, a revolutionary idea, or a miracle product—we soon find ourselves in need of rescuing once again. And just when we think we've destroyed the villains that threaten our happiness—whether those are "toxic" people, bad habits, or personal flaws—we soon find new villains (that are too often resurrections of past ones). Our inner drama seems to have unlimited sequels.

Perhaps you know someone who is prone to idealizing new lovers—thinking each new admirer is The One, The Saviour, The Soulmate. Perhaps you do this (or have done it in the past). In such people, you will notice an important, correlated behaviour: making villains out of past lovers. Those who idealize also demonize. Those who judge some people as good also judge other people as bad. Those who glorify retirement also vilify their working life. Those who idealize money tend to blame their poverty for more problems than it causes. Every hero needs a villain. To call something holy presumes the existence of evil. Claiming that some people can save us presumes that others can destroy us. Labelling some part of our experience as acceptable presumes that other parts aren't. In these all-too-common judgments, we can find the roots of imbalance.

Classifying the world into good and evil is addictive. To defend your ideas about what is good, you must continue to find what is bad. To fuel your disdain for what you call evil, you must place your hopes and dreams into what you call holy.

Like this, we get stuck in the same old cycles with the same old personalities. We think that the answer is to eliminate so-called toxic people from our lives, yet whether we like it or not, those people also exist as characters in our inner conversations. Walking away is rarely enough. To change the cycles, we need to change the narrative.

One of my most influential villains was my first boyfriend. Our relationship ended in a full-scale war. I hurt him, and he hurt me. I was his villain, and he was mine. If I ever felt a pang of regret for my actions, it buckled under memories of what he had done the week before. I always felt justified. Then, my retaliation would become his justification. Round and round we went. Every offense I detected against him scored more points on my victim card. And every reason he found to call me crazy allowed him to neglect his own mental health issues. We both became addicted to conflict. Sure, we both said we hated it. We both said we wanted it to stop. But we needed those fights to fuel our distorted stories about the world.

Where did these cycles originate? Of course, my ex and I didn't meet each other thinking we'd degenerate into mutual abuse, but there were warning signs. For example, even as a teenager, I had come to believe that some men were good and others were bad. The bad men, like the ones who had hurt me, were selfish, angry, callous, and greedy. The good men, like the ones I dreamed about saving me, were self-sacrificing, creative, sensitive, and generous. My ex had his heroes and villains picked out as well. The bad women were needy, irrational, crazy, and demanding. The good ones were kind, smart, open-minded, and accommodating. When we met, we saw only the "good" in each other. For the first few years, the illusions held strong. Inevitably, reality crept in. The "bad" began to show. Disillusionment. Disappointment. Blame. The more we vilified one another, the less we could see those beautiful things we had appreciated in the first place. It seems tragic that two people could end up distorting one another so much, but the truth is that we'd been distorting each other all along. Our mutual denigration had its roots, once upon a time, in mutual idealization.

Some of these judgments, we internalized from the world around us. (Romance novels and pornography certainly didn't help.) But our narrative about good and bad was also shaped by painful experiences. Many of our judgments originated in self-protection.

After we get hurt, it's natural for us to try to prevent future pain. In crisis situations, it often seems more important to keep ourselves safe than it does to be accurate with our interpretations. For example, if you sent your child to a daycare center where one person abused him, you might generalize that the whole daycare is dangerous. This seems to make sense. Better safe than sorry, as they say. What could be the harm in making sweeping generalizations? Yet this same line of thinking causes us to formulate prejudices about ourselves and others.

Self-protection may lead us to demonize our self-communications instead of decoding them. We may label some voices as "wrong" when their messages are integral to our well-being. After rejection, we twist ourselves into pretzels trying to be what other people want us to be. After disappointment, we take care not to get too excited or have too many expectations. But isn't rejection vital communication about how our opinions and actions relate to the rest of the herd? Sometimes, it might help to stick with the group, but other times, breaking away from the pack is essential to individuality. Rejection can pave the journey of authenticity. And doesn't disappointment give us valuable insight into our needs? If we feel excited about something that doesn't work out, then the more disappointed we feel, the more we must have wanted it. They say you don't know what you've got till it's gone, but disappointment shows you how you *might* feel about something being gone before you ever get it! Our so-called negative emotions—fear, sadness, anger, disappointment—are important feedback mechanisms.

Self-protection can also make us lock away our "good" parts to shelter them from "evil." If vulnerability leads us to hurt, we might put walls around our tenderness to keep it safe from attack. Thus, we lose contact with that voice. Its foils—perfectionism and ego—become mental dictators. This kind of self-preservation can be the most dangerous of all precisely because it appears to be so self-compassionate. We start to believe that our most beautiful parts are our weakest, yet they are only weak because they are unused and inexperienced, locked up in our inner towers seemingly for their own good. In the meantime, we wait for saviours to end our suffering and ruminate on the villains who locked us up in the first place. All the while, the keys lie in our own pockets.

Self-preservation is hasty. Efficient. It asks, "What hurt us?" and "How can we avoid it in the future?" This voice has been part of the human experience for millennia. It protected us from predators. It is not in the habit of consulting with others about its decisions. It picks something to blame and sticks by its choice. This can cause us to internalize answers we had previously dismissed. For example, my parents warned me that people shouldn't be trusted, but this was meaningless to me until I got hurt. In a moment of pain, self-preservation demanded to know what was happening. My parents' answers were waiting.

Like this, we develop prejudices. A child is not born hating anyone. Still, he is not deaf to the influence of the outside world. The people around him might vilify certain beliefs, races, or cultures. He might learn these prejudices and emulate them. Once he becomes old enough to think for himself, he can start to question these beliefs. But if he gets hurt by one of those so-called villains, the fear-driven stories will sink in their claws. Self-protection is a powerful motivator. It turns fear into hatred. It turns shame into narcissism.

We cannot suppress our self-preservation instinct, and we cannot ignore the narrative of the outside world. Of course, self-awareness can help us look beyond right and wrong, but the moment we feel pain or fear, our ancient voice of survival will try to convince us to hide, attack, hate. No one is immune to this. It affects people who practice self-awareness as much as those who do not. Maybe you could take some pill to suppress it, but why would you need to? After all, if everyone has self-protective tendencies, and there are happy people in the world, surely there must be a way to respond to these impulses in a constructive way! This is what self-awareness can do. It will neither halt automatic responding nor prevent it, but it *can* give us the power of choice. Self-preservation is like an anti-virus program: it seeks for threats and tries to destroy them. But somewhere in that process, a little screen pops up to ask, "Do you agree with doing this recommended thing?" The room for choice already exists. All we have to do is seize it.

This is especially important for healing trauma. After abuse or neglect, we believe that blaming those who hurt us will liberate us from suffering. And for a moment, it does. If you spent years thinking that everything was your fault, then pointing the finger back at your abuser will bring a much-needed perspective: it wasn't your fault. This is true. But just because something isn't *your* fault doesn't mean it must be someone else's. Pointing that finger can bring us a moment of peace, but keeping it pointed can have devastating consequences. We can trap ourselves in the very cycles we're trying to escape.

Recognizing that someone is mistreating us is a crucial part of the healing process. Many children of abusive circumstances have no idea about the gravity of their situation. When we have only one version of the story, we believe that this is how things are for everyone. Only when we begin to see other perspectives—by hearing about other people's childhoods, for instance—do we start to ask questions. Was that fair? Was it okay? Did I deserve it? At this point, anger often flares up. It wasn't fair! It wasn't okay! I don't deserve to be treated that way! Anger is a healthy part of the process. It comes in to counterbalance our helpless feelings—shame, guilt, desperation—with a dose of assertiveness. Anger says, "We don't have to put up with this anymore."

At this point, self-protection steps in. As soon as we realize that someone has hurt us, this voice demands to know what happened. What hurt us? Why? How can we prevent it from happening again? Here, we face some life-altering choices. How we answer these questions can either facilitate or obstruct the healing process. Tragically, we might come from multiple generations of people who, through those same choices, tried to stop the cycles but ended up perpetuating them.

Self-protection wants quick solutions, efficient ones, but healing is not so easy. The people who abused us become characters in our inner conversations. They influence our other voices. Fear turns into anxiety. Shame turns into self-loathing. Doubt turns into addiction. Even if the person who taught us these patterns died, we would not be free. Healing is a long, hard road of adjusting our inner voices to match reality as well as integrating them with each other. On that road, there are no shortcuts.

Vilifying the person who hurt us is an attempt at a shortcut. On the surface, it seems like a one-way ticket to self-liberation. But behind the scenes, imbalance begins to take root. One person might look with disgust at her abuser and swear that she will never drop to the same level. This might keep her from becoming a bully, but it also traps her in perpetual victimhood. Whenever someone becomes angry around her (like non-abusive people also do), she vilifies that person. This strengthens her self-concept. "At least," she thinks, "*I* am not like *you*." Another person might look with disgust at his past self and swear that he will never be a victim again. This might keep him from being abused, but it also traps him in perpetual antagonism. Whenever someone tries to advise, guide, or manage him (like non-abusive people also do), he vilifies that person. He strikes back. This also strengthens his self-concept. "I don't let anyone treat me that way anymore," he thinks. Both people are trapped. They see themselves and others as characters, objects. Unconsciously, they keep casting the same roles. They become trapped in the very stories they are trying to escape.

When I left my parents' house as a teenager, I had several truckfuls of emotional baggage. My approach for the difficult years was to count down until they were over. I learned this from a counselor at school. She said, "You can't change other people, but you can leave as soon as possible." I yearned for that day, gasped for it. When I left, I thought I was free. I left behind my villains, and my ex left behind his. We had spent so long demonizing our families and worshipping each other; we both thought this was it. We thought healing was leaving. We thought we'd live happily ever after.

Shortly after this move is when everything began to go sour—when our mental versions of each other fell off their white horses and began plotting sinister plans. At the time, this seemed like a coincidence. It wasn't. The stories we had learned from our childhoods included a villain. As long as we had someone to oppose, we dressed each other up as heroes. But when we left town together, the villain costumes we had stuffed our relatives into laid crumpled on the floor. Sooner or later, the show had to go on. Someone had to put on the villain suit.

Some people say that this pattern—glorifying and vilifying people—is a property of sick people with an incurable mental disease. But we all distort each other to some degree. We're all predisposed to this sickness because it runs not in the blood but in the inner conversation.

Even those who come from peaceful families internalize the hero-villain drama from mainstream media. And those who grow up around parental conflict are even more vulnerable. They invent stories about why it's happening, whose fault it is, and how their own relationships will be different. To them, the media's fairy tales are narcotic. Then, heartbreak strikes. Or rejection. Or humiliation. When our inner conversations are full of human caricatures, what else can we assume? We begin to judge, to hate, to divide the world into "us" and "them."

We can begin to heal ourselves and our society by identifying the actual poison: the narrative. We internalize the judgmental conversation of the outside world, and we allow it to shape our inner one. Then, our actions cause other people to embody the same story. On and on it goes. We cannot heal judgment through judgment. The only way out is through understanding.

When I stopped waiting for someone to save me, I stopped putting people on pedestals. When I stopped simplifying others' actions into evil intentions, I stopped hating people. When I stopped thinking of myself as a chronic victim, I stopped dodging responsibility. And the one responsibility I'd been avoiding more than any other was this: healing from past abuse. The long way. The hard way. The sustainable way.

Those with a victim self-concept sometimes react with fury at the idea that they need to change anything about themselves. This is understandable. To them, it sounds like the bully's taunting: "Change yourself. It's your fault. Something is wrong with you." But *every* person needs to examine his or her inner conversation. Every person. No matter if that person has abused, been abused, or never seen abuse.

Awareness is an essential part of healing. No one deserves to be reduced to a two-dimensional label. No one deserves to be mistreated, objectified, or hurt. This is why it's so important to heal these wounds instead of trapping ourselves in self-protective misunderstanding. The sooner we heal our traumas, the sooner we liberate ourselves from the people who hurt us. By hating them, we hold onto them. Thus, we cannot heal. We can walk away from our real-life villains, but we cannot walk away from the villains in our heads. As long as we demonize some part of the human experience, we will continue to distort reality. In some form, the cycles will continue. And we, as the victims, will be just as blind as our bullies. Just as helpless. Just as unconscious. Without awareness, we allow our judgments to manipulate us.

These same distortions make us more susceptible to consumerism. Think of the self-help schemes you've fallen for in the past: the fad diets, the 10-step books, the fitness trends, the life overhaul methods. You might feel embarrassed about believing that these tools would work, but you were *not* making conscious choices. This kind of marketing is so hypnotic because it capitalizes on imbalance. The most effective advertisements make a villain out of some part of you, and then sell you on a hero. The ad says your stubborn fat is the reason you're unhappy, and this magical pill is here to banish your suffering. It says your negative thinking is ruining your relationships, and this subliminal positivity tape will make you more charismatic. It says your acne is ruining your self-image, and this cream is here to make you confident. This framework is an emotional Molotov cocktail. If advertisers can convince you that some part of you is wrong or broken, they create an inner villain. How could you not buy into their hero? In such situations, your decision appears to be "buy the product or not," but it's more like "be fat or be happy," "be negative or have friends," "have acne or be confident." It's a double bind. Both options assume that you can't have both. Moreover, both options assume that these things are "problems" you can't fix without a magic pill. If all that doesn't tip you over the edge, they ask, "Do you want to pay $30 now or $100 later?" It's irresistible. We click "Add to Cart."

We can resist such manipulation—not through will-power but awareness. If you do not vilify any part of you, then nothing is a so-called problem. Each physical and mental state is simply a self-communication. Extra fat is not bad. It is an important message. Maybe it's your body talking about your diet or your thyroid talking about hormone levels. The same goes for acne, negative thinking, cellulite—anything people try to eradicate. No one can convince you to vilify a part of your experience that you deem necessary. And if you don't aggrandize any part of you, then nothing is a saviour. If you already have a relationship to your confidence, happiness, and acceptance, no one can tell you stories about them. And no one can sell them back to you.

There will always be those who try to use people's imbalances for profit. They do this out of experience, not malice. Filmmakers make movies about heroes and villains because they sell. Marketers push emotional buttons for the same reason.

Here, we stumble upon a painful, yet encouraging, fact: self-help was never to blame. Marketing was never to blame. In the opening pages of this book, I assured you that my goal was not to undermine the authorities and experts who milk your insecurities. Now, you can see why this would be futile. If you denounced the people who have taken advantage of you, nothing would change. You might free yourself from the dogma of one authority, but soon enough, you would fall into another. Our inner drama cannot end with the victory of the hero or the destruction of the villain. These are merely the beginnings of future sequels. Only peace, not triumph, can end a war.

The Names We Call Ourselves

One major obstacle I had to overcome in writing this book was my first book. The ideas I had once domesticated hissed and growled at each new perspective I invited into my mind. My self-concept dragged around my past work like a ball and chain. Every time I glimpsed the naked truth dancing toward me, my self-image sighed. Sure, that could be real, but I can't say it. Look at all these things I said before. It was exhausting. For almost a year, I couldn't write a word.

My liberation came in the form of an epiphany: I had no obligation to be consistent. If the ideas in this book happened to contradict those in the first, then readers could watch my awareness grow. How was that something to be ashamed of? I left the ball and chain behind. Inspiration flooded my pages with courageous words unencumbered by yesterday's counterparts. Soon enough, I hit another wall. On the one hand, I was saying, "Trust yourself. Look within. Don't seek answers on the outside." On the other hand, I was writing a book about this, which necessarily exists outside any person who reads it. My self-concept grappled between being a person who trusts the greater patterns of life and a person who teaches them. Between having faith and taking leadership. The two felt incompatible. I was stuck here for months.

I found freedom in another realization: my faith didn't need to leave the room when leadership entered. Both trains of thought could coexist. In fact, they could work together to formulate new ideas. The words rushed forth again. But more walls came. All in similar forms. All with similar cures. Every step along my journey toward truth, I have been tormented by paradoxes in my self-image. I have fought for a consistent character to show to the world.

Trying to maintain a uniform self-concept seems like a harmless thing to do. In fact, this is what most people believe it means to "find yourself": to find out what kind of person you *are* as opposed to what kind of person you are not. Inside each of us is a conversation of paradoxical voices speaking to one another in tangled patterns. But instead of labelling the voices themselves, we tend to label ourselves *as* them. We define the leading characters in our inner dramas as our characteristics.

Often, we define ourselves by whichever voices are loudest. If you often experience anxiety or self-doubt, you might define yourself as anxious or unconfident. This is like seeing a movie starring Will Smith and walking out of the theatre convinced that you *are* Will Smith! It makes no sense, but we do this for a reason: we yearn for a sense of identity. There is nothing wrong with this desire. In fact, you can use it to your advantage. Because you crave to know yourself, you can consciously feed heaping spoonfuls of reality to your self-concept. Thus, your self-image can facilitate your relationship with truth instead of impeding it.

How do you define yourself? You might say you're responsible, quiet, or creative. You could call yourself unselfish or unassuming. These labels can be just as limiting as the meanest self-talk. There is a difference between labelling an inner voice and labelling yourself. When you notice an inner pattern and call it something (responsibility, for example), you have the room to find contrary patterns (such as playfulness). However, when you notice an inner pattern and call *yourself* that ("I am a responsible person"), you shut off communication with contradictory voices. You get stuck looking at yourself through one perspective. You begin to play a role. Even the most harmless-looking defini-tions can limit you.

For example, if you call yourself generous, you might not easily admit how you hold back. You might also find proof of your generosity in situations that don't merit it. Moreover, it can become hard for you to receive. If you always have to be the generous one, no one can give to you. Because giving makes people feel good, your insistence on being The Giver makes you hog this good feeling to yourself. You might also find it difficult to give unconditionally. When you need to give to yourself but give to others instead, your gifts may come with expectations. Then, your recipients might feel awkward or even manipulated. You, in turn, might feel resentful about their lack of gratitude. On the other hand, choosing self-care when you feel drained replenishes your ability to give out of genuine kindness rather than obligation. Oddly enough, calling yourself generous can make you much *less* generous than you'd be otherwise.

Allowing paradoxes into your self-concept is an un-comfortable process. We tend to see the world in binary terms: yes/no, go/stop, either/or, on/off. There is no option for both. I am either outgoing or shy. I'm either artistic or business-minded. I'm either generous or greedy. If I repress an inner voice, I reflexively base my self-concept on a voice that counterbalances it. For example, if I suppress my crea-tivity, I might identify as an analytical person. If I stifle my need to be around people, I might identify as a hermit. Likewise, if I fixate on some voice, I shun those with oppos-ing perspectives. For example, if I focus on my anxiety, I might call myself anxious while ignoring my capacity to be calm. If I idolize my emotions, I might call myself passionate or intuitive while ignoring my voice of reason. Binary think-ing impedes understanding and healing. When we find some undesirable characteristic, we believe the solution is to flip the switch: to stop being negative and be positive instead. To stop being a people pleaser and be assertive. But whichever way we flip the switch, we ignore some part of reality, which encompasses *both* perspectives.

The best version of you is the *real* you, not some role you've assigned to yourself. You encompass all the characters in life's drama. This is what makes you so versatile, so dynamic. You can look through the eyes of all your inner voices and explore the rich diversity of reality. Why limit yourself? Identifying with any voice is like choosing a permanent position for your light switch. If it is always off, you can never have light. If it is always on, you can never have darkness. Either way, you will be dissatisfied.

When we neglect our inner paradoxes, self-observation becomes more difficult. We seek justification over truth. We waste precious time and energy defending our self-concepts. For example, if I say I'm stupid, I will dismiss my best ideas. Yet if I heard those same theories coming out of someone else's mouth, I might call her smart! If someone turns the same ideas I had once discounted into a million-dollar business, would this make me suddenly realize my intelligence? Of course not. I must confirm my self-concept. Thus, I will take this situation as further proof of my stupidity. I'll say, "I was too dumb to act on a good idea." On the other hand, if I call myself smart, I might ignore the ideas and behaviours in myself that I'd label as stupid in others. Then, if someone brings these tendencies into the spotlight, do you think I'll suddenly become humble? Of course not! I will applaud myself for being *so* smart that I know when to do the very things other people should never do. No matter what I call myself, it is a trap—an imaginary world far from reality.

As long as we keep insisting that everything is either one way or another, we will not be able to see the truth. As long as we keep labelling ourselves as being something and not something else, we cannot see ourselves. At worst, we can become delusional and paranoid. We tend to think of people who warp reality as being insane and ourselves as sane, but reality distortion happens on a spectrum. It isn't an on/off switch either. We all distort reality to some degree. As long as we share the same narratives as those around us, no one questions our mental health. When our distortions detach from our culture's dogma, then it becomes a "problem." Yet the so-called problem walks hand-in-hand with all of us from moment to moment. Every silenced inner voice makes us slightly more delusional. Every glorified inner voice makes our ideas a bit more unrealistic. To keep hold of reality, we must welcome and embrace its paradoxes.

Anytime you look at yourself from one perspective, you will find proof that counters it. Every characterization comes with holes and inconsistencies. We cannot avoid this. We can, however, choose how we react to those contradictions. Will we allow opposing ideas to lie down with the ones we believe are true? Or will we treat every piece of evidence that conflicts with our beliefs as an enemy attacker? Until we make a purposeful effort to do the former, we will unconsciously continue to do the latter.

Our need to justify our personality traits makes it easy for other people to come along and seduce us. For example, if I self-define as stupid and someone wants to sell me a product, how can she convince me to purchase it? By reminding me that I'm slow and proving that she's not. Of course, not verbatim! Even if I call myself dumb, I'd probably not appreciate hearing it from someone else. But there are subtle ways to send the same message. First, they say, "Aren't you tired of running around in circles, never getting anywhere?" Then, they say, "For the past ten years, I've been getting results for people just like you." It's hypnotic.

Of course, that pitch would not work on everyone. If I self-define as smart, then I might have an inflated view of my achievements and a more-than-healthy level of cynicism about expert advice. But while certain marketing tactics couldn't snag me, others would. If I see myself as someone who never makes mistakes, this becomes my weakness. If someone can convince me that all smart people buy his product, then I have no choice. And if he convinces me that not buying would be a mistake, then I'm hooked. I might believe that I'm making a smart, conscious purchase decision. Really, I am making an automatic decision to rationalize my self-concept.

We can categorize these kinds of labels as "binary beliefs." Each time we choose one, we alienate another. Most of us carry hundreds of binary beliefs about ourselves. Thus, we give opposing labels to "them": the people we believe to be different. And we project our beliefs onto "us": the people we lump in with our own characteristics. Because *all* these labels are generalizations, we distort "us" as much as we distort "them."

For example, I might call myself introverted. I will then project my beliefs onto those I call introverts—regardless of what those people are truly like. Even if *my* introversion shows up in a certain form, this doesn't mean other people experience the same thing. Curiously enough, they might never admit it. If we go to an "Introverts Unite" meeting, we will reinforce one another's beliefs. Even if I noticed inconsistencies between what others call introvert traits and my own experience, why would I bring them up? Doing so would only poke holes in my self-concept and alienate my new tribe. Like this, I'll distort myself as well as my new comrades. And when I meet people who exhibit the traits I've labelled as extroverted, I will see those people only through that label. I won't understand them because I'll think I already do. Every label I give to myself affects my views of *all* other people.

On top of our binary beliefs about ourselves and others, we also have binary judgments: who is bad and who is good, who is wrong and who is right, who is the hero and who is the villain. Together, they compose persuasive myths about us and them, me and you, this and that. As time goes on, these interpretations impair our ability to make conscious choices. For example, I might think of myself as hard-working and label my foils as lazy. I might also believe that being hard-working is good, while being lazy is bad. Thus, I become a hero, whereas "the lazy people" become villains. Then, I will try to discover who these lazy people are. Does laziness flourish in a specific race, age, or gender? I will formulate my prejudices. Then, imagine how I'll treat those people. Imagine how much harm I can do while telling myself that I'm right—that I'm doing good. And the damage does not stop at other people. If I insist on always working hard, think of the things I might not allow myself to do: take breaks, stop when something feels wrong, think before taking action. In the long run, my beliefs can harm not only my relationships but my physical and emotional health as well.

It's important to note that our self-concepts do not dictate our judgments. I could think of myself as hard-working while demonizing hard work. Likely, I would alter my labels to allow for these judgments. I could self-define as a workaholic and define my foils as easy-going. Or I could think of myself as a neurotic perfectionist and think of other people as wise realists. Thus, I could criticize myself and put my foils on pedestals. As you might imagine, I'll feel chronic envy for those people: them over there who have it all figured out. I might not be cruel to them, but I will disrespect them nonetheless. Have you ever had someone assume that your life was perfect and problem-free? It isn't a compliment. It feels like a judgment. (Because it is!) Combined with the psychological impact of chronic self-criticism, these beliefs can be just as harmful as their opposites.

The words "hard-working" and "workaholic" can refer to the same behaviours. So can "lazy" and "easy-going." As you discover the names you've given to yourself, you will find paradoxical characteristics and paradoxical judgments. Realize that there is a difference between the two. Opposing perspectives, behaviours, and patterns exist. We can observe that. We can see one person's silence contrasting another's talking. We can observe a set of behaviours as assertive and another set as submissive. On top of these observations, we layer our judgments. We can say, "He is listening patiently, and she is blabbing on and on." About the same situation, we can also say, "He's clammed up and unsociable, but she's charismatic and outgoing."

It might seem like the solution is to use non-judgmental language. We could say, "He is quiet, and she is loud." This seems like a fix, doesn't it? We can label other people with *observable* characteristics instead of judgmental ones. Yet this kind of labelling can be the most dangerous of all. When we consciously make an effort to see more of reality yet ignore the paradoxes within each person, we are, in a way, worse off than the people who don't care much for seeking truth. We live the lies with more conviction.

The trouble with saying things like "He is quiet, and she is loud" is that these are often assumptions. They are not descriptions. All we can observe is that those people appear to be acting this way *at the moment*. Of course, you might say, "He is quiet, and she is loud" and mean just that. It isn't about the words themselves but the perception of the person speaking them. The same goes for talking about yourself. You can carefully choose each word, avoid judgmental labels, and never follow the words "I am" with an adjective while still harbouring a static self-concept. On the other hand, you can say the most imbalanced-sounding thing—for example, "I'm a good person"—and still maintain inner balance. To you, this phrase might allude to the daily choices you try to make rather than describing a personal characteristic. Balance isn't about using the "right" words. It's about perception.

Those who seek to remove their binary judgments without removing their binary beliefs often find themselves moving through waves of conflict. Trying to withhold judgment in the long term is nearly impossible when we continue to sort the world into stagnant categories. For example, imagine that you self-identify as a homebody, and so do I. However, I think it's wrong to be this way, while you think it's the best thing to be. We get into many fights about it. I try to convince you that going out is the right thing to do. I blame you for holding me down—supporting me in being the worst version of myself. You, on the other hand, advocate for staying in. You blame me for sucking the enjoyment out of our perfect lifestyle. One day, I have an epiphany. I become aware of my binary judgments. I say, "Okay, it's not good or bad to be a homebody or a social butterfly." Like this, I win back some self-esteem. Of course it feels better not to think of myself as a bad person! But there is one thing I have not addressed: my desires to go out. If I continue to stay in every night while having urges to meet new people, I can only withhold judgment for so long. Eventually, my distaste for our lifestyle will return. Then, I will probably feel even *more* bitter toward you because, as I withheld judgment, your perspective dominated our relationship. Like this, we will keep having the same fights. Until I shed my binary characteristics, my judgments will keep resurfacing.

And until I stop distorting myself, I am bound to keep distorting you.

Our binary labels reinforce toxic relationship dynamics. People with extremist self-concepts often gravitate toward one another because they both distort reality in similar ways. For example, when you call yourself weak, you push down your inner strength. Because you've alienated it, you do not have a relationship with that voice. Thus, you can't accurately detect it in others. You might *think* you can pick out a strong person in a crowd, but your conceptions of strength are bound to be idealistic. How can they not be? If I tell you stories about my friend Amanda, you'll imagine her. In your head, she'll have a certain age, race, gender, clothing style, hair colour. If I give you no information about her appearance, you'll imagine her any way you please. Even if I tell you a thing or two, you're still bound to be off the mark. Only when you *see* her, you can imagine her properly. Without the feedback of experience, you cannot calibrate your assumptions. Thus, when you identify with one voice and repress another, you are bound to have inaccurate, unrealistic ideas about the repressed voice. Then, you might gravitate toward the people who repress what you express. Their personification of your silenced voice *is* unrealistic because it's unbalanced. Thus, it matches your distorted ideas about it.

You might call yourself weak and repress your strength, but what is "weak"? Maybe you define weakness as being emotionally reactive, not speaking up for yourself, and letting other people influence your behaviours. Based on this self-definition, your idea of strength—which you claim not to have—might be someone who acts aloof, self-advocates, and doesn't bend to others' expectations. If you meet someone like this, you and that person have something in common: you idealize and demonize the same behaviours. You both think showing emotions is wrong. You both think it's better to do what serves oneself over what serves others. You both think it's right to advocate for what you want. But these values you both share are embodied in the other person, not in you. In this relationship, you will *always* be wrong. However, this person is not to blame, and neither are you. The harm lies in the labels.

If you were to polarize and start repressing every emotion, advocating for every desire, and letting no one influence you, you'd find something interesting. You would lose valuable parts of your life that you had taken for granted. For example, you might find that pushing down your painful emotions also numbs your joyful ones. Or you might discover that having a thick skin in public makes you more volatile behind closed doors. And if you tried voicing your opinion in every situation, you'd find your relationships crumbling. You'd realize that, sometimes, holding your tongue is a crucial skill. And if you insisted on always doing things your way without anyone's influence, you might develop anxiety about making the right choices. In short, you'd discover that what you call strength comes with its own emotional, mental, and social consequences.

Now, imagine shedding your binary beliefs and judgments. You could acknowledge that you often experience emotions, withhold your opinions, and follow others' lead. This is one part of you. It is not good or bad, and it does not exist alone. You are also capable of self-expression, stoicism, and leadership. Even if these voices are quiet, they are still there. You can work on bringing them to the surface in situations where they can serve you. For example, you might work on voicing your opinions in important discussions, reacting less to people who disrespect you, and showing your creative side more often. These skills might take you years to practice and refine! Yet the effort itself will bring you closer to the truth. By releasing your binary judgments *and* your binary personality traits, you can explore the full realm of your potential.

From your new mindset, imagine how you'll react to unfeeling, unyielding people. You won't put them on pedestals! By experiencing your inner paradoxes and bringing them to peace, you won't fall for the charms of a person who is off balance. This applies to a myriad of other labels. If you call yourself dumb, you might admire people who parade their intelligence: reciting facts, engaging in debates, and trying to outsmart others. After you liberate yourself from these labels, you might realize two precious things. First, what you call intelligence also exists within you, and this pattern has its limitations. Second, what you call stupidity is a collection of other voices— wonder, playfulness, emotions, creativity—and these perspectives are not only valid but also important! After such epiphanies, imagine how you'll feel when you meet people who exhibit intellectual superiority. You will no longer feel inferior to them. With inner balance, you can heal your self-esteem and avoid toxic cycles with others.

Simply by acknowledging our inner foils, we avoid making a personality out of them. If I claim to *have* two perspectives, then how can I claim to *be* either one? I cannot. No matter how many times you've looked at the Big Dipper, you've never obsessed about *being* the Big Dipper. Simply by pointing and saying, "I see some pattern," you imply that you are lying in the grass looking up at it. Thus, redefining your characteristics as inner characters can help you hear your inner conversation—all of it. Not only the parts that torment and seduce you.

This, too, is a process of addition. No binary belief is wholly false. It is merely a piece of the truth. Our task is to balance our one-sided beliefs with other viewpoints. If I find proof that I sometimes make the right choices, I can no longer think of myself as someone who always screws up. If I find my capacity to be assertive, I can never again call myself a pushover. If I view myself as a beautiful piece of nature, I can never again claim that I am ugly—even if my reflection continues to spark these thoughts!

Balancing our inner voices is similar to overcoming prejudice. When you've been fed ideas about some group, you're vulnerable to perceiving every person from that group through those ideas. You think, "All of them are always this way." Inevitably, you will find a few examples to prove your stereotypes. When we find proof, we assume that we've found the truth. It might seem like the solution is to prove the stereotypes false—but they aren't! Few things are always false or always true. It wouldn't help to flip the switch by thinking, "None of them is ever this way." This perspective is just as extreme, just as inaccurate. Instead, the open-minded say, "Some of these people are sometimes this way, like all people." Removing prejudice is a practice of dissolving extremism. By inviting contrasting ideas to cohabitate with our existing ones, we can have a more balanced mindset.

Every act of self-definition is an act of self-limitation. Of course, we must limit ourselves from time to time. When someone asks you for your name, it wouldn't be helpful to reply, "Hello, I am an interconnected part of the universe." That person was asking you to describe yourself as a separate entity from others. This is okay. Limitations are sometimes necessary. But if limiting yourself is *all* that you can do, then you will experience a poverty of understanding. Your task is not to cut out your self-limitations like malignant tumors but to expand your awareness beyond them. Thus, they lose their power over you. They become small cogs in a larger machine.

As you begin to enrich your self-concept with all of reality's paradoxes, you will feel less certain but more peaceful. As you allow each moment to be as diverse as it is, you will stop fighting with it. You will begin to understand. You will begin to live.

Balance's Vocabulary

When our inner conversations are imbalanced, we might assume that our lives are imbalanced also. This is rarely the case. Without inner balance, we become participants in the great balancing act. The voices we repress show up in other forms: desires, worries, dreams, pains.

A balanced conversation is like a seesaw. With inner balance, I can put my voices on each side and let them play. I am complete within myself. However, when I identify with one voice, I cannot fill up both sides of the seesaw. I sit on one end. I wait. I crave for someone or something to sit on the other side. When my partner comes, we start to play. Back and forth, up and down. We become stuck in those cycles. This is the basic anatomy of both addiction and conflict. We might play this game with a person or a substance. In any case, awareness gives us power. Instead of interpreting such urges literally, we can learn to translate them as words in balance's vocabulary.

Sometimes, we interpret our self-communications about imbalance as feelings of attraction toward certain people. Specifically, we might feel drawn to those who speak with the inner voices we ignore. As they say, "Opposites attract." Yet this does not apply to everyone. If I allow for paradoxes within me, how can any person be opposite of me? Even extremism is halfway to balance. Thus, it might be more accurate to say, "When we identify with one role, we might feel attracted to people who play the opposite role." But that just doesn't have the same ring, does it?

Balance is life's director. When I take an extreme role, its foil is left uncast. In the absence of a balanced protagonist, the director will cast a supporting role. Through balance's tricks, we keep ending up in toxic relationships. We wonder why it always happens to us. We identify with one part of a balanced dynamic and alienate the other, yet the rejected part ends up in our lives anyway. We cannot run from balance. We can only avoid inner equilibrium.

For example, imagine that you always listen, and I always speak. Thus, you have trouble with self-expression, and I have trouble with empathy. We might meet at a party and end up talking to each other. Why wouldn't we? I would annoy people by not letting them get a word in, and you would bore them with your silence. Then, we'd find each other. You would listen, and I would speak. While this would be an uncomfortable situation for many people, you and I would feel at ease. We'd fill each other's voids. Like this, we become dependent on other people. We feel like we need them because we believe they have something we don't. When people complete each other's imbalances by role-playing, it is like a tango. The dance has certain steps; we just follow along.

When balance coaxes you toward your foil, you invent stories about why you're attracted to that person. You say it's this quality or that attribute. These things you have in common. Really, you are being controlled by an automatic impulse as ancient as the human nervous system and interpreting it to have some rational basis in reality. Balance is moving through you, shifting the voices in your head like marionettes while you tell yourself you're in charge.

However, feeling attracted to someone who sits on the opposite side of your seesaw is not necessarily a path to codependency. It is a *signal* of imbalance, not a promotion of it. The message of any emotion is not a direct order but a reflection of how things are. To figure out what this communication means about how things *could be*, you must take it in context. If you and that person are both interested in learning from one another, you could cultivate inner balance together.

Awareness is power. If you can observe balance pulling at your strings, you can break free of your dependence on others. For example, if you suffer from chronic anxiety, you might feel drawn to wise gurus whom you see as enlightened, detached, peaceful—opposite of you. Then, you might pay these gurus massive amounts of money to help you become more like them. But what if you reacted to your admiration in a different way? You could ask, "What role does balance play in this emotion?" You can then observe how the guru's peacefulness counterbalances your stress. Instead of trying to emulate her, you could seek out the inner voice she represents. You can use your attractions as guideposts for self-discovery.

Learning to interpret our self-communications better gives us the power to make different choices. If we decipher our desires, we can choose how we fulfill them. For example, imagine that you've been in a happy relationship for 20 years and, suddenly, you get the urge to cheat. You can say, "Okay I see that. What else could this mean? And what role does balance play?" Here, you might discover something interesting: you feel bored, not only with your partner but also with your daily life. The urge to cheat might be a desire to counterbalance your routines with some excitement. Or you might realize that you feel unloved and misunderstood. The attention of a new lover would counteract your loneliness. Or you might find that you're vilifying your partner and making a saviour out of someone you just met. There are hundreds of ways to interpret your urges. At the end of the day, you must relate your self-communications to your unique situation. Maybe the urges *are* sexual and nothing more. No one can tell you how to interpret your self-communications or how to respond to them. The important thing is to realize that you are, in fact, interpreting them and that balance dynamics influence your interpretations. The more aware you are, the more informed your decisions can be. Not all desires are literal.

We might also seek balance in substances and experiences. For example, for many years, I could only fill my mind with ideas, not empty it of them. I believed every thought that rolled through my head. I could never just *be*. I *had* to think. And I liked this about myself. I called myself analytical, intellectual, smart. But I had a weakness. When it came to drugs and alcohol, I couldn't help myself. I said I had an addictive personality. Back then, after my first glass of wine, I would feel like a different person. Alcohol would free me from the endless barrage of thoughts that never left me alone. The more I drank, the freer I felt. Why wouldn't I drink until I vomited and passed out? Looking back, it makes perfect sense. Every drink was a way to uninterpret reality— something I desperately needed to do. After I stopped doing drugs, I also stopped drinking for a while. In those months of sobriety and self-discovery, I learned to detach from my thoughts without any crutches. I learned to empty my mind. Some months later, I decided to have a drink. That was a profoundly strange experience. It wasn't the same. It didn't feel as good as it used to. It didn't start a cycle of drinking more and more. Now, I can have a few drinks and stop, like most people. I don't force myself to stop. I stop because it's enough. I don't have to fight with myself not to drink every day or at every occasion. It's simply not necessary. This is the relationship that most people have (and have always had) with alcohol. Some blame the substance. They say it's evil and inherently addictive. Others blame the people. They say, "Once an addict, always an addict." I disagree. Maybe it is this way for some people sometimes, but not for everyone always. It certainly wasn't for me. When I lived on one end of the seesaw, I needed alcohol to come and play with me. When I filled up both sides myself, it lost its addictive potential.

Instead of condemning ourselves as hopeless addicts, we can try to understand *why* we crave certain things: how we achieve balance with our most toxic behaviours. If we assume that comfort comes from outside ourselves, we will search for it in clothes and TV shows, labels and facts, bread and sugar. But if we find comfort within, we stop searching. The same goes for love, understanding, acceptance. When we think these things come from other people, we become addicted to approval and attention. When we discover our own potential to be the lover *and* the beloved, we stop grasping for others' reactions. We find completion within ourselves.

We might also experience our imbalances as aversions. Sometimes, we hate our foils. Or we love them one day and scorn them the next. Hatred is still a relationship. Feeling hostility or resentment toward someone keeps that person in our lives, in our minds. We don't need to *enjoy* playing on balance's seesaw to participate.

For example, if I call myself boring, I might yearn for an exciting person to complete me. Yet I might also hate so-called exciting people because they make me feel inadequate. Or I might hate those I label as boring because they reflect me back to myself. Or I might adore them because they make me feel like I'm not alone. My reactions to people who exhibit certain characteristics will change depending on my self-concept and my judgments. We can hate seeing ourselves in others as much as we might love it. At the end of the day, violent rejection is not much different from hypnotic attraction. When you bring two magnets together on one side, they stick. On the other side, they push each other away. Each imbalanced conversation dynamic within us is a powerful magnet. Whether we push or pull, it still indicates the same thing: polarization. When we react in extreme ways to others, this indicates our own extremism.

When we demonize a person or a group, we tend to gravitate toward people who feel the same. Instead of unconsciously seeking our foils, we might seek allies. Knowing we are not alone in our extremism gives us comfort, yet this can be a dangerous game. Uniting in hatred brings out humanity's darkest tendencies. It can also make us tolerate mistreatment from our so-called comrades. Because we are so busy waging conflict with the opposition, we neglect the horrors that happen on our side—even when we are the ones who commit them.

Our extremism might lie not only in our feelings about people but also in our impulses to act a certain way around them. We might feel pressured into a role because someone is playing its foil. For example, if I am always easy-going, this will create friction with some people. After all, there's a time and a place to be easy-going. Sometimes, it helps to be serious. If you come to me and say, "There's a problem," how will I respond? I might say, "It's okay, don't worry about it." Chances are that this would make you worry *more*. You will perceive the absence of my concern and reflexively fill the void. I could approach the same situation by saying, "Yes, that sounds valid, what can we do?" Likely, your response would be less extreme. I am concerned, and so are you. Knowing that you are not the only person dealing with the situation, you can relax a little. Yet this also works in the other direction. If you worry about every little thing, I will unconsciously fill the void where relaxation should be. With other people, I might not be so dismissive, but with you, I'll have learned to be this way.

Even the most unaware person feels like something is not quite right in a seesaw relationship. Because we have the capacity to carry all of reality's paradoxes, limiting ourselves to one small part feels suffocating. Thus, our adoration for someone might give way to disgust. We think we are fed up with a specific person, but we cannot claim to "know" the people who play on our seesaw. We only know the roles they take with us. Our disgust is not for them. It is for our automatic reactions. We tire of role-play.

When we escape our foils, we believe we are free. Yet the next time we become intimate with someone, the same cycles might repeat. While nothing can prevent us from meeting people who assume polarized roles, inner balance helps us interrupt (and even avert) our toxic cycles with them.

Before we continue, I want to address the elephant in the room. There is a tempting assumption to be made from this kind of thinking: that we attract all mistreatment to ourselves. Let us take a moment to pick apart this logic because it can mislead us down a path of self-blame and shame.

When you sit on one end of any seesaw, you will experience urges to put something on the other side. Like this, you might find a partner. But sexual attraction is by no means the only way that balance speaks to us. Our self-communications about imbalance are simple, and we dress them up in whatever complexities are available in the moment. Suppose that you begin to experience a never-ending stream of judgmental thoughts. If you grew up around drugs, you might counterbalance with substances. If you know someone who is laid back, you might crave to spend time with her. If you were raised by a critical parent, you might emulate these behaviours and discover that criticizing other people takes the pressure off you. Your environment plays a major role in how you interpret your signals of imbalance. It dictates what's available to you.

There are those who self-identify as people pleasers, yet they have never fallen into a relationship with someone who takes advantage of them. There are people who deny their assertiveness and submit to others, yet they have spent their lives being supported and loved. Sometimes, we're just in the wrong place at the wrong time.

Just because our misfortunes have a *relationship* to our imbalances does not mean we *asked* for them. A person who is lacking in self-love and desperate for a saviour can meet someone whose unconditional affection teaches her to love herself. Or she could fall for someone who mistreats her. Or she could gather a supportive circle of friends. Or she could craft stories out of her desires and become a world-renowned novelist. Or she could end up in a cult. Our desires do not determine the exact contents of our life stories. Balance and imbalance show up in all kinds of forms.

Another risky assumption is that each physical and mental ailment must originate from self-repression. Of course, each time you inhibit some essential part of yourself, there will be symptoms, but this doesn't mean that *all* symptoms come from imbalance. It would be nice, certainly, if we could cure the world of cancer and schizophrenia by asking the meek to concede their assertiveness and the mathematicians to draw once in a while. Alas, the inner conversation is not merely emotions, behaviours, and thoughts. It is also chemicals and genes. You are a whole universe of causes and effects—some you can control and some you cannot. Balance is an important pattern, but it doesn't exist alone.

Throughout these pages, we have limited our exploration to emotions, thoughts, and behaviours. The point is not to ignore realms over which we have less control. Rather, you will learn what you cannot change as you focus on changing what you can. While you are busy seizing opportunities for growth, that which cannot grow will remain as it is. Thus, you will have the opportunity to accept it.

If you plant a hundred seeds in poor soil and nothing sprouts, you may cry at the failure. If, instead, you plant those seeds in fertile soil, some will still fail, but you will not cry because you will be too busy nursing the seeds that have sprouted. Self-awareness is that fertile soil. It does not remove failure; it helps you cultivate your potential despite it. Thus, you can stop dubbing yourself a poor gardener.

Inner Balance

Allowing foils to coexist within you creates a kind of wealth: a richness of possible reactions. Every voice is useful in some situations and not others. Thus, when any situation occurs, you can consult the part of you that's most likely to be helpful. With inner balance, you can live a fuller life instead of only playing one small part in it. If you can only perform one role, balance will typecast you in life's grand production. You will be there only to shine a light on someone else's character. But if you can play *all* the roles, you can stage an entire performance by yourself. No one can limit you. You can shine by yourself.

You don't have to wait for anyone or anything to save you. You can become your own therapist, partner, and best friend. You can break your dependence on quick fixes, relationships, and material things (including books). And it begins with trust. Trust that everything you need—every saviour, every helper, every answer—is within you.

Think of a person you would say is supportive. Maybe you are fortunate enough to have such a person in your life. Or maybe this is someone from the past, from a book, or even from your imagination. Now, think of someone whom you'd never call during a crisis. You've likely met a number of such people, and probably still know a few. Ask yourself this: what decides whether a person is supportive or unsupportive? Words? Actions? Feelings? Dig a little, and you will find the answer. The knowledge of what kind of support you need is already within you.

But what does this knowledge mean? When someone supports you, what happens? Here, we can find balance at play. Giving support is a matter of restoring equilibrium within another person. Before the healing moment, there is often balance *between* two people: one feels calm, and the other feels pain. In a moment of support, balance moves to being *within* those two people. Each has his or her own work to do. The suffering person must make some space for the supportive person's compassion, and the supporter must make room for the suffering person's sorrow. Balance gives an invitation. Both people must accept it. From the outside, it may seem like the helper is doing all the work, but the distressed person is doing just as much.

Some people get addicted to being balanced by others. They cannot support themselves. They move from therapist to therapist. They drive their friends away complaining about their problems. They make their families uncomfortable because they're always in a pit of despair. They put themselves on one side of the seesaw and wait for someone to come and play. After they vent to a friend or a therapist, they feel better. But the next time they become upset, they need another friend, another therapist. How can they learn to balance themselves?

Self-support begins with a realization: when others help us, they do not bring anything new into our experience. Every person has triggers—not only for negative states but also for positive ones. The people you call supportive simply push your existing buttons. They speak the words your inner voices long to hear.

You can trace your successes and failures with supporting others to the same patterns. You might recognize your experience in another person, or you might not. You might have the same emotional buttons as him, or you might not. It is not only a matter of awareness and communication; it is also a matter of chance. No matter how much you want to help others, they live in private worlds. You cannot decipher a person's triggers at a glance. Unless, of course, the person you're looking at is yourself.

You have already played the supporter, and you have played the supported. You have both roles within you. Now, you can invite these voices to speak to one another. If you can contain the process of receiving and giving help within yourself, then you can learn to push your own buttons. You can nurse your own wounds. You can facilitate supportive, healing conversations all by yourself. Healing, for our purposes here, is not something mystical. It is simply the process of calibrating to health: restoring inner balance through awareness.

In every moment, balance is pushing you toward external things, searching for peace. You can learn to interpret these same urges as opportunities to self-balance. For example, if you are addicted to receiving other people's support, each strike of desperation is an opportunity. Your emotions are crying out for a safe space to be heard. You crave the attention of another person because that's how you've been meeting this need, but the need itself does not specify a deliverer. You want to be heard, accepted, loved. You could take this as an opportunity to hear, accept, and love yourself. You could journal your thoughts. You could hold yourself while you cry. You could tell yourself all the soothing things that would calm you down if another person said them.

Containing the cycle of support within oneself might sound unsatisfying to a person who is dependent on others. I have been such a person. I didn't believe it would feel as good. How could I support myself when I had a history of destroying and hating that same self? It seemed like a recipe for neglect. But those moments when I ran into my own arms were more intimate than I could have ever imagined. With other people, I was never completely satisfied. No one said the very things I wanted to hear at the very moments I wanted to hear them. No one else could read my mind. I could.

Inner balance doesn't mean that we need to live our lives alone, never receiving support from others. It is not a recipe for solitude. It is simply a mindset: we acknowledge that everything we observe outside ourselves also resides within us. Like this, the love we receive can teach us to love ourselves. We can learn self-support from those who support us. Rather than becoming dependent on those people, we can learn from them. Thus, we can become such a person to ourselves.

Let us look at an example. Imagine a woman who suffers sexual trauma. In the name of self-protection, she puts her body behind protective bars. Her mind takes over. In some ways, this serves her. She dives into the world of thoughts and ideas. She constructs an identity around her intellect. All the while, any suggestion of a sexual situation sends her into a panic. She becomes uncomfortable with displays of sexuality around her. In intimate situations, she turns away from touches intended to be gentle and caring. Without realizing, she triggers insecurity in other people. Over time, she recognizes that she has some work to do. She tries to explore her sensual side. But without a balance between her mind and body, she simply emulates the images of female sexuality from the media. This attracts her to people with similar imbalances: those who objectify her as much as she does herself. These interactions only polarize her further.

Now, imagine that this woman becomes attracted to someone who feels connected with his sexuality. He helps her feel safe enough to explore herself. She begins to open up. Here, she has a choice. Will she perceive his help as salvation or education? Saviour seems a more romantic label. "I love you; I need you." Are these not the words of a million love poems? But if she sees him as a saviour, she does a disservice to them both. The more she experiences momentary balance with him, the more she will crave it. She will need him more and more. Her desperation will trigger another balance dynamic: chase and run. The more she attaches, the more he'll detach—not because he is a "bad person" but because playing saviour is suffocating. Any human being is more than a provider of services for another.

Instead, what if our hypothetical woman takes the healing moments in the relationship as lessons? What if she allows her experiences with her new lover to spark self-discovery? She might start to dance, paint, play, stretch. She might unearth aspects of her unique sexuality that even her lover couldn't have known about, and she could teach these back to him. She can love him without needing him. Thus, she can give him the space to be a human being. Then, she can explore *his* sexuality too, which would be impossible with him always playing the role of explorer. And maybe this man has a repressed relationship with his intellect. Thus, they can help one another reach balance. He can help her reunite with the sensations of her body—with that voice suppressed seemingly for her own benefit. And she can help him reunite with his potential—with that voice torn down by society's judgments. Like this, the relationship could serve them both.

This is one example of healing. It doesn't mean that all similar traumas require the same process, and it certainly doesn't mean that the tale is over. There are countless levels of balance and imbalance: multi-layered networks of conversations interacting with one another. There is always more work to do.

There is a difference between healing through balance and "healing" by way of extremism. The latter is much more common than the former. Instead of inviting our inner voices to get along, we tend to throw one voice off the pulpit and replace it with its foil. Thus, imbalance sways in the other direction. At the time, it feels like liberation. Yet we remain imprisoned by the same old cycles.

For example, when I self-defined as a victim, I sorted people into three categories: fellow victims, villains, and saviours. Time after time, everyone I put on a pedestal would fall off. Every saviour turned into a villain. Eventually, I got sick of it. I went through what I thought was a profound personal change: I rejected my victimhood and proclaimed my strength. I stood up for myself and refused to be taken advantage of. I went around trying to save people who idealized me—people whom I soon disappointed. It seemed to me that my life was so different in those two time periods, but I was still stuck in the same old drama. All the while, I had the potential to hurt others as well as be hurt by them, to help people as well as be helped. When I recognized this duality—and not a second sooner—I swallowed two difficult ideas: I was hurting myself, *and* I could save myself. Until I accepted myself as someone who needed help *and* someone who could provide it, I could only blame others, depend on them, and use them. To cultivate intimate relationships, I first had to become intimate with myself.

Switching between extremes is common, and it's something to watch for as you learn to balance yourself. I say "watch for" rather than "prevent" because, sometimes, the only way to balance a plank on a ball is to let it sway back and forth until it reaches the center. It is not altogether dangerous for someone who has spent a lifetime being docile to experience rage, but it *would* be dangerous for that person to identify with rage and hold onto it. We must learn to sit quietly in the director's seat, watching our inner voices rather than jumping on stage to take their roles.

Imagine a man who comes from generations of submissive men with controlling partners. With every generation that inherits this imbalanced conversation, there is an opportunity to heal. He tries to break the cycle by polarizing to the other side. Instead of refusing his desires, like his father did, he indulges in them. Instead of sacrificing himself for those he dates, like his grandfather did, he becomes assertive and authoritarian. Instead of attracting dominant partners like his mother, he ends up with someone submissive. He thinks he has broken the cycle. Yet he is still stuck. Instead of playing his father's role, he plays his mother's. He has simply flipped the switch from one binary position to another. Then, his kids might try to break the cycle by polarizing, yet again, to the other side. Nothing would change for the better. But what if he practiced self-awareness instead? He could embrace both roles. He could integrate his father's imbalance with his existing mastery. Yes, mastery, because this man has not been doing anything wrong. He has simply been doing half the job. By allowing for assertiveness *and* submissiveness in his inner conversation, he can have wholeness within himself. After reaching a state of inner balance, he might attract a partner who self-balances as well. The cycle would be broken.

The more traumas we have experienced, the more difficult it can be to achieve inner balance. Overcoming self-protective reflexes can take many years. But do not let this discourage you. You could spend those same years strengthening your robotic reactions. Every moment of awareness counts.

Your inner conversation is like a dense forest. Your inner truth seeker can climb a tree and look down to see the big picture. This perspective will give you valuable insight, yet it might also give you vertigo. We are used to being the voices in our heads, not watching them. We are used to playing the characters in our mental dramas, not directing them. To experience ourselves from a bird's eye view is a shock—the height alone triggers terror. But we must not run away. If we allow our fears to control our actions, we only strengthen the voice of self-protection and, truth be told, that voice is already strong enough. Wrapped in a blanket of illusory safety, you cannot be free.

The first leg of our healing journey, we spend paralyzed. We watch ourselves doing the same old thing, unable to stop it. This is normal. We begin deaf. Then, we learn to listen. Then, we gain the ability to speak. Pressuring yourself to take action right away would be like forcing yourself to sleep in the daytime. The day has another purpose. As do the early phases of awareness. Paralysis teaches you to embrace uncertainty, build curiosity, and practice acceptance. What a gift. Life keeps you from speeding through her lessons.

Of course, having inner balance doesn't mean you must act in dualistically extreme ways all the time—happy one day, depressed the next, domineering next week, then servile by the end of the month. You don't need to devote half your behaviours to one extreme and half to the other. You also don't need to find the midpoint between all extremes and act from there. When I talk about having inner balance, I am not specifying how you should *act*. I am referring only to having an *awareness* of the foils within you. That awareness may or may not translate to your behaviours.

Instead of seeing yourself as a responsible person, you can embrace your potential to be responsible as well as your potential to be playful. Of course, you might still have a deeper relationship with the voice of responsibility than its carefree counterpart. This is fine. You do not need to take 43 risks for every 43 responsible actions! With inner balance, you might still choose to act responsible 95% (or even 100%) of the time. But, whatever you do, it will be by choice, not habit.

Accepting your inner voices allows you to stop role-playing with others. To pacify your external conflicts, you must wage peace, first and foremost, within yourself. Every time you encounter an opposing opinion or unfamiliar viewpoint, you can accept it as an invitation to acknowledge some part of you. Even if one in every million people has some perspective, it is a part of the human experience. To have inner balance, we only need to accept that it exists within us. If one in a million people is a mass murderer, for example, acceptance does not mean that we must murder anyone or imagine doing so! We only need to recognize our own capacity for violence. Why would we do this? Many people refuse. They believe some people are evil, and we must fight for justice. But there is a world of difference between a person who believes she is pure good fighting against pure evil and a person who approaches so-called evil with an understanding of its origins, causes, and relationship to the larger picture. Those who fight for peace without inner peace can only wage war. The self-proclaimed heroes keep the villains alive.

If you listen, you will find both peace and violence within you. Even if you choose never to act on that violence, awareness will keep you balanced. Your peaceful actions will include compassion for people who do violent acts. You may disapprove of their actions, but you will understand that they happen for a reason. You may work to pacify violence, but you will do so without vilifying the people who undertake it. Like this, you can create a more peaceful world. Your actions will come from harmony, not heroism. Your peacekeeping will be an externalization of your inner peace.

Resolving external conflict is not so different from resolving your inner one. As you work to unite your inner paradoxes, they will resist. If two voices have been waging war within you, they both need to grow. Your job is not to eradicate one and glorify the other. Just like you cannot abandon yourself as you are and ask for a new version, you cannot simply cut and paste patterns within your experience. You also cannot control them. As it is with children, if you try to force your inner voices, they will find a way to evade you. Your task is to help them mature: to hear them, understand them, and put them into situations where they can learn, grow, and develop better relationships with one another.

Self-balancing is like being a relationship therapist to your inner voices. If you were counseling a couple, you might encourage the quieter one to speak and treat her with kindness when she does. Like this, you not only invite her feedback, but you also set an example for how she should be treated. Naturally, you teach the louder partner to listen better. You help both of them evolve without pushing, forcing, or silencing.

By being the third party to two conflicting voices, you introduce an essential ingredient of conflict resolution: curiosity. When two people polarize into opposing roles, they cannot understand each other because they are unwilling to hear new information. As the observer of a conflict (rather than a participant in it), you can invite wonder. For example, the part you call "heart" might resent what you call "mind": the way it clambers on about this and that, judges you and everyone else, keeps you up at night. Instead of internalizing this resentment, you can ask questions. Why *is* your mind so active? What could it mean? You might discover a simple cause—for example, you drink too much coffee. Or the story might be more complex—for example, you've woven a sense of identity around your thoughts, and you're afraid of mental silence. You can investigate thoroughly and embrace whatever you find. A supportive counselor remains open, understanding, and impartial. You can acknowledge each inner voice without unconditionally believing it. Like this, you can facilitate profound changes.

Your healing conversations might be long and exhausting. They can get messy. When you first coax the voice of strength out of your inner basement, you might be unnecessarily harsh when speaking to others. Or you might cry for hours after saying one declarative sentence. Both are okay. At first, the voice of judgment might allow compassion to speak for only five seconds before interrupting. This is still progress. Each time you try to balance yourself, you learn something. Even if a conversation shifts right back to how it was before, this is not a failure. With each attempt, your inner truth seeker becomes wiser. Every time you practice, it matters.

As you bring two voices to peace, you might begin calling them by the same name. They might "become one" in your experience. Of course, this is not literal. There is inhalation, and there is exhalation. They are different, but in your perception, they unify into the process you call breathing. Likewise, as you heal the relationship between two voices, you may choose to label the conversation between them instead of only labelling them separately. Like this, you can integrate them with other parts of you. For example, you might refer to the balance between interpretation and uninterpretation as "thinking." Then, you can work on harmonizing this pattern with others, such as your body or your emotions. You might also need to dismantle a voice into smaller conversations to address imbalances at other levels. For example, to harmonize your mind and your body, you might first need to bring your body to peace by balancing nutrition and exercise. There are infinite levels of patterns. By keeping your labels fluid and your mind open, you can explore as many of them as you can.

The process of balancing—the process of healing—is never finished. After you help a couple resolve some conflict, they will still have other issues with each other and with themselves. As you balance one part of your inner conversation, you will find imbalance in another. And every dynamic you heal can fall out of balance again! It is never over. Even inner balance is not a mountain peak. It isn't something you become like a caterpillar becomes a butterfly. Even the most self-aware person sometimes identifies with her inner voices, judges herself and others, and becomes stuck in certain roles. Imbalance happens. Self-balancing is a lifetime job. This might feel stressful at first, but as you embrace dynamic reality and release quick-fix thinking, the stress will melt away. Healing will become a way of life.

Conversations That Heal

For a seed to achieve its greatest expression, it must come completely undone. The shell cracks, its insides come out and everything changes. To someone who doesn't understand growth, it would look like complete destruction.

CYNTHIA OCCELLI

I spent much of my childhood feeling like a helpless victim. I was afraid of my own shadow. I cried almost every day. After a few heartbreaks, I built up scar tissue. I grew to believe that emotions were the enemy. My inner bully pushed my inner victim into a locked vault in the basement of my heart. There, she stayed for years. I stopped crying. I grew cynical. I became disgusted by vulnerability within myself and others. I constructed my self-concept around intelligence, strength, and tenacity. I hid away in an armoured fortress, ready to attack anyone who came too close. People often called me intimidating. It was music to my ears. I thought I had found the perfect solution to avoiding pain. In those years, I did horrible things—not only to others but also to myself.

I remember a friend saying to me: "My sister is like you. She's tough as nails, and that got her through a lot. Then, our mother died. My sister tried to deal with it like she always does, and it didn't work. Sure, I was a big mess for a while, but I'm okay now. She's still not. Being tough only gets you so far."

That conversation ominously foreshadowed what happened in the following months. My inner victim began to revolt against her imprisonment. Memories of unhealed traumas overtook my mind. Nightmares. Insomnia. Anxiety. The part of me that I thought was a pathetic little weakling had grown, over the years of isolation, into a terrifying force. I couldn't deny it any longer. I had to accept that this part of me existed. It was like unlocking Pandora's Box.

My mind split in two. This was one of the most painful experiences of my life. My inner victim came tearing out of her cage and accused me of being a monster. An abusive narcissist. In return, my inner bully called me a pathetic weakling. An attention-seeking crybaby. I had only ever played one role while projecting the rest of the story onto other people. To experience both felt like insanity. And maybe it was.

I called in sick to work. I spent the best of three days in bed. The victim cried, "How could you?" Memories came like a typhoon. People hurting me. Me hurting people. Me hurting myself. In return, the bully hissed, "You worthless waste of skin!" The insults were never-ending. Too sensitive. Weak. Pathetic. I felt self-pity *and* self-hatred at the same time. I wanted to protect myself from harm, but I wanted to hurt myself too.

My thoughts spiralled. I couldn't sleep, couldn't eat. Choking on hysteria and anger, I felt darkness in my blood. I felt broken, perverse, irreparable. I did the only thing I knew how to do, the thing I'd been doing my entire life in response to pain—I ran. I ran as fast as I could. There were moments when I realized just how serious my inner turmoil had become. On a lonely morning after a three-day drug binge. On a subway train after I passed out and missed my stop. For a split second, I would touch the tornado of helplessness and destruction that was ripping me apart. Those moments didn't last. As soon as I could, I would run to whatever escape mechanism was most accessible. It wasn't until years later that I recognized those precious seconds of perceiving my inner reality as self-awareness.

I was running full speed from the war raging within me, but I couldn't run fast enough. Every night, if I slept at all, I had nightmares. I started hallucinating voices. Something was always moving in the shadows. Sobriety was terrifying. Suicidal thoughts wrapped around my mind like boa constrictors. One day, I couldn't run anymore. To escape the battle between the voices in my head, I walked to the ledge that would have killed them both. Only there, I realized there was another way.

In the helpless silence where I almost gave up, I heard something else: a voice that compelled me to detach from my thoughts, to learn about who I was, to face my fears. Where did this voice come from? When I have told this story in the past, some people have ascribed mystical, magical qualities to my realizations, saying these ideas came "from beyond." At the time, it did seem otherworldly. In retrospect, however, I see that I had been unconsciously learning self-awareness for years. In my last year of college, I encountered the idea of mindfulness. At the time, I called it useless fluff. That year, I also read *Zen and the Art of Motorcycle Maintenance*—a book that soon became my favourite of all time, though I couldn't explain at first why I had liked it so much (or even what I had learned from it). Also, a few years prior, I had read Victor Frankl's *Man's Search for Meaning* for an Art and Psychology class. Ironically, I found little meaning in it at the time. I struggled to welcome new information into my worldview. I didn't welcome it, but clearly, I didn't ignore it either. Fragments of wordless words lay outside the walls I had built around the violent drama raging within me. My inner war became so aggressive that it tore those walls down. In the ruins of my fortress, I looked out, expecting to see an endless void. Instead, I saw a little package waiting for me. It was bursting with ideas that I could never have understood from inside my mental prison. Once I overcame my stubborn resistance to opening it, the contents of that package, like fragrant oils, saturated the rooms of my mind with insight. I realized that I was an interconnected part of everything around me. I realized that thoughts were some-thing I *had*, not something I *was*. I admitted that I was an addict. I acknowledged that I had some traumas to heal. I had to stop hiding and running. I had to face myself.

Like this, I came back to where I had started: the vic-tim and the bully. But this time, I wasn't paralyzed by their conflict. The voices themselves were no different. They were still fighting with each other and fighting to survive. In some ways, they were worse. In my self-avoidance, I had de-stroyed my adrenal health. My body couldn't help me deal with stress. I had stopped drinking and doing drugs. I had no escape. I was an emotional mess. The bully would rage, de-fend, resist. The victim would cry, wallow, brood. But I, for once, did not identify with either role. I didn't have to be-lieve every insult or defend myself against every accusation. Instead of participating in my inner conflict, I started observ-ing it.

I began to write every time I had intense emotions, and I had many. I discovered that there was a world of dif-ference between writing to vent and writing with awareness. Writing to vent—something I had been doing for years— meant identifying with some voice in my head and speaking its words. Writing with self-awareness, however, meant al-lowing the voice to express itself while keeping a bird's eye view on whatever it said. On paper, the two were indistinguishable. The difference was my mindset. Instead of reacting to each angry thought and using it to feed further anger, I let myself become curious about it. I began to understand that my aggression came from a desperate need to protect myself from the dangers of the world. Likewise, instead of reacting to each helpless thought and using it to feed further self-pity, I explored deeper. I saw how my feelings of depression linked to self-avoidance. Once I was no longer chained to my thoughts, I could see them as phenomena—like a scientist observing bacteria in a Petri dish. What I saw amazed me. The bully and the victim had so much in common: a strong sense of injustice, fear of pain, blame, exaggeration of past situations, blind self-preservation, and a lack of responsibility.

Slowly, the two became one. The dams of the victim's sadness burst with fury, and the bully's ironclad facade split with helpless sobs. The tears and rage came together in a tirade of emotion. One moment, I'd be furious. Then, I'd start crying. One second, I'd feel hurt by someone's ignoring me. Then, I'd feel angry at my helplessness, then ashamed of my anger, then frustrated about my shame. On and on. I started to feel like I was holding space for a tantrumming, little child within me. I started to label these episodes as my inner child. As I became more proficient at accepting, allowing, and observing my emotions, I trained my inner adult. In the middle of a journal entry in mid-2012, the voice that had been listening to all my emotions suddenly spoke. Here's what I wrote:

People have treated you badly in the past and I want to be better. I want to take care of you.

You'll never be lonely. I'll smile for you. You'll never have to hear insults or about all that's wrong. You don't need to constantly be reminded of your flaws.

You don't need them to validate you. Let me. Let me make you feel good. Let me take care of you.

I'm sorry for what I've done to you. I'm sorry for feeding you drugs and alcohol and sweaty men who didn't give a shit about you. I'm sorry for all the times I looked at you and told you that you were fat, ugly, that you would never be anything to anyone.

I'm so sorry for taking you to all those places.

I'm sorry for all the wasted time, the wasted brain cells, the wasted moments when you could have been shining. I am sorry that I tried to make you evil, dark. You are not evil. You're not dark.

You're not that.

You are not a shadow. You are not a character. You're not a party girl. You're not like that.

You are beautiful and smart and funny and shy and real.

You really like everything to do with food.

You love making people happy. You love helping.

You like being appreciated.

You want to feel like you matter. No one can give you that more than I can.

It was my job to start with. I've just fucked it up. Give me a chance. Give me a chance to love you, beautiful girl. Let me be good to you, because no one was, and sur-

round yourself with anyone and everyone who agrees. But that's second.

Let me. Let me do this. Let me love you.

Fuck the boys. Fuck them. You. Me. That's what really matters. This. Us. This is forever. This can and will be beautiful.

I promise.

Trust me.

I still tear up every time I read this. That voice was the loving parent (and partner and friend) that I so desperately needed: a strong, compassionate being who could protect the vulnerable parts of me. As I began to listen to this voice, I realized that this letter to myself was not the first time it had appeared. I dug through my old school notes to find a crumpled piece of paper that proved this voice had already been around a few months prior. It was there during the downward spiral that led to my breakdown. Here's one of the things it said:

> *You know, this feeling may pass and I will likely forget all about it and think that this note is not real, only the pain is. But, just now, for one second, I felt like everything would be okay. Remember that you can still feel that next time you're thinking about leaving this world. You'll be okay, Vironika. I know you. You're strong and beautiful and you've got life by the balls. Never forget that.*

I did forget, but I did not ignore. Those words remained somewhere deep inside an old binder as much as they remained deep inside my mind. When I revisited old journals, I found this voice emerging from time to time, speaking to me in the third person: telling me everything would be okay, telling me to remember what I loved rather than what others wanted from me, reminding me to love myself.

At first, I was shocked by how frequently this voice had tried speaking to me. I thought I had discovered self-love in the aftermath of my suicidal struggles, but I hadn't. My supportive inner voice had been there for as long as I can tell. Every time I watched a movie where one character said to another the words I was desperate to hear, I'd feel something release deep within me. Every time I found myself across from a person who was ignoring or mistreating me, I'd beg silently for what I needed most. Every time I allowed myself to be vulnerable, I'd feel better at hearing certain words and worse at hearing others. I already had all the information I needed to comfort myself. The potential for that voice had been there all along, like a seed. It just needed fertile ground.

I continued to write every time I felt upset. After I expressed my feelings, I would skip a few lines and give my compassionate voice the chance to speak. It would say, "It's okay to feel this. It won't last forever." It would say, "You're going to be okay. No matter what, you've got me by your side, and I'll be here to protect you. We're in this together."

Those conversations changed my life, not only because they began the process of healing childhood wounds, but also because they gave me a chance to practice love, leadership, and empathy. The more I spoke to myself in a loving way, the more I could speak this way to other people. The more I acknowledged my own symptoms of self-avoidance, the more I could notice and forgive them in others. Slowly, I became to other people who I had become for myself: a helper, a healer, a leader. To be a voice of love in the world, I first had to practice speaking to myself with that voice. My inner light needed to practice illuminating my own darkness; otherwise, I would've never had the courage to light up anyone else's. I had to start with me.

Like this, the adult became a coach, and the child became a client. My job description changed to "life coach," and I took on clients. I didn't pay to advertise my services; I simply shared my story, my insights, and my fears. I spoke with the voice of experience, and those who felt that voice open up something inside them would open up to me. I learned in the first few years of coaching that it was more effective for me to work with people whose inner conversations mirrored mine. I also realized how important it was for people to question their thoughts instead of always believing them. For some, this awareness remained concealed in unopened packages outside their inner fortresses; and I have painstakingly learned that mental walls are not something we can help people break down if they do not want to.

My inner coach grew quickly, but I grew in other ways too. With each client I supported on the healing journey, I also healed. As people showed me their deepest fears, their most traumatizing memories, their most embarrassing mental tendencies, I recognized myself. Each recognition brought me peace. "Oh," I would think, "I'm not alone in having felt like this!" or "I'm not the only one who still struggles with this!" These conversations continue to change my life. Each person I meet on this journey is a new friend for the once-lonely voices in my head. As I facilitate the healing conversations of others, I facilitate my own. I have unwrapped the gift of a painful past to receive a sense of purpose. Self-awareness has helped me grow into myself.

But it's not always easy, and there is always more work to do. Last year, an article of mine about the importance of giving people with mental illness more than just medications went viral, twice. The first time, it received kind praise from supportive people. The second time, it received cruel criticism from people who picked apart, twisted, and mocked everything I said. After this second wave, I felt devastated. The voice of my inner child cried out from deep inside me. As usual, the adult came to the rescue. I cried. I raged. I took care of myself. This helped for a few hours, but then the pain returned. I tried to self-support again, but the weight on my chest felt irremovable. The wound wasn't healing. This went on for weeks. Every morning, I woke up feeling lifeless. Every day, I would cry, journal, and talk to my partner, Jamie, about how I felt. It didn't help. My inner child was in crisis. The adult tried to give support, encouragement, kindness. It wasn't enough.

I tried to reframe the situation. I thought about how the article probably wound up somewhere on the internet where my critics (as opposed to my fellow voyagers) gather. My work had reached people who either didn't understand it or didn't agree with it. That is bound to happen. The diversity of life guarantees that this will happen to any person, any idea, and certainly any piece of writing. I knew this. I told myself this. But I didn't feel any better.

Weeks passed. I tried another approach. I worked on cultivating more compassion for the commentators. I wrote kind responses to even most abusive comments. That helped a little, but not much. I wasn't feeling particularly resentful toward those people in the first place. Something else was wrong. I tried another approach. I tried to learn some valuable lessons from the situation. I learned, for example, that it is important to state the obvious when dealing with controversial topics. Although it was clear to me that I wasn't telling people to go off their meds, some readers misinterpreted my words this way, and I could have helped clarify that. I also decided to share my experiences with my tribe. Maybe, I thought, I felt unsupported because hundreds of strangers had criticized me, and I hadn't been courageous enough to ask my community for some balancing kindness. I reached out. The outpouring of support I received was incredible. It was unlike anything I'd ever experienced. I cried. I thought the wound had healed. I felt better for a day or two afterward. Then, the discomfort returned. Nothing was helping.

Months passed. I felt anxious and depressed more often than usual, and I slowly fell out of touch with many parts of my work. I continued coaching and looked forward to each session, but I stopped writing articles and rarely visited my online communities. I told myself that I was taking the space to heal. Then, one day, I received an unexpected rejection in my email inbox. Her words reminded me of those article comments. I felt deeply triggered, but to my surprise, when I went to journal, I thought, "I'm fine, just leave it; let's do something else." This was serious. I finally admitted that the onslaught of rude comments on that article had traumatized me. I wanted to heal that trauma. But when I tried to approach it, I felt strong urges to revamp my website plugins and get my taxes in order—anything to avoid feeling the pain. Later on that same day, someone in one of my Facebook groups wrote that he wasn't the same person after a blog post of his received a blitz of negative comments. My inner child, through pursed lips, groaned in frustration. She had something to say.

I lay down and shut my eyes. I beckoned my inner child to speak to me. At first, she refused, but after some gentle encouragement, she suddenly screamed, "How could you?" I watched in horror as memories flashed across my mind: flashbacks of childhood emotional abuse alongside that letter where I promised to love and protect myself. My thoughts screamed, "You fucking promised!" One part of me glared angrily at another. I hadn't experienced this kind of inner conflict for years. I didn't know what to do.

I sat down to write. I tried to let my calm voice soothe my emotional one. But instead of loving and supportive thoughts, I had only defensive and frustrated ones. Yes, I promised. Yes, I thought I could protect myself from harm, but then I wanted to save the world too. To be a leader. To be more than just safe. I *knew* that would involve criticism. My inner adult had run out of compassion. She had done everything she could, and all she received was ingratitude. The feelings of inner battle, once again, raged full force.

I kept trying to heal this conflict, but self-awareness was not some miracle that fixed the pain. It kept me off the ledge—I didn't hurt myself or anyone else—but I was exhausted and sensitive. How could I heal a conversation that was not happening? Neither voice would speak to the other, nor would they speak to me on paper. There was a cold wall between my mind and heart. I felt helpless. My journal pages were blank.

Later that week, an epiphany came as I was talking to Jamie about this situation. Somewhere in the middle of an irritated sentence, I said, "I'm just so angry at myself." It sounded familiar. "How could you?" Flashbacks. Memories. Accusations. This had happened before. It dawned on me: what if my inner child was angry with *herself*? What if this voice had split, once again, into bully and victim? What if that conversation had fallen out of balance again? I hadn't realized that this could happen, but the more I explored this possibility, the more I felt it was true.

Sure, logically, I had accepted that leadership would come with criticism. I thought I was prepared. But my emotional self, like any real person, had her delusions. She acknowledged that criticism would be necessary while dreaming of the possibility that it wouldn't be—because that's what she was promised. Shattered idealisms fractured my inner child into an angry bully who blamed her for having those hopes in the first place and a helpless victim who defended her right to have dreams.

Understanding was my bridge to a healing moment. As I realized what was happening, I felt a deep sense of self-compassion return. My inner adult wrapped her arms tightly around her beloved estranged half. My mind and heart called a truce and sat on the floor of my soul in a crumpled heap, crying in each other's arms. One part of me sobbed, "You promised" while the other whispered, "I know. It hurts, I know." And then, there was peace.

Since then, I've had countless rough days with myself. I've also had countless healing moments. When I first shared this book with reviewers, my inner conflict flared up in response to the critical comments. Yet the more criticism I have received (and the more pain it has caused me), the more I have been able to heal myself. Each time I have held my emotional self through her outbursts, she has become stronger, wiser, and calmer. Slowly, I've learned an important lesson: self-love and self-protection are not the same thing.

Conflicts, traumas, and roadblocks happen. That's life. But every struggle is an opportunity. Each time I become unbalanced, it is a new puzzle to solve, a new labyrinth to traverse, a new landscape to explore. Compared to some people, I am experienced. Compared to others, I am a novice. And any skills I have, I learned in difficult, painful times. Without experiencing imbalance, how could I have learned to heal it? So the only Happily Ever After in the story is this: I am content to participate in the eternal conversation of life moving through me and helping that conversation move through others. I may never be healed; but each day, I am healing. My work is never finished, but I have grown to love working. My life is my art.

The Truth Seeker

I have set out to come upon a new me, to open to the things that have long beat with their insistence at my door. I do not wish to surpass anyone or anything. I pray only to outgrow myself in emancipation and consciousness. I stipulate nothing, save that I grow. I know the price and I will pay.

MURIEL STRODE

✖ ✖ ✖ ✖ ✖ ✖ ✖ ✖

Living without self-awareness is like sitting in a room with advisors running in and out, giving you instructions. One comes in and yells, "Let's get working! We don't have enough time!" You believe her and start working. After she leaves, another advisor storms in and says, "Wait! We don't have a plan. We can't work until we make a plan." So you start making a plan. As soon as the door swings behind him, the first advisor bursts in again. She screams, "Why aren't you working? We're supposed to be working!" On and on. The advisors never acknowledge one another's existence. Over time, both become frustrated about not getting their way. This is how it is in most people's minds. Is this how it's been in yours?

All along, there's been someone in the middle of the room: your inner truth seeker. Through the eyes of self-awareness, you can see that neither advisor is qualified to make decisions alone. They need teamwork. They need leadership. So you can call your inner voices together and create a space for them to resolve their differences. You can listen to them, give them opportunities to use their talents, and help them work together in peace. This is the art of talking to yourself.

Your inner truth seeker can help you discover, heal, and understand your inner patterns. But when you first find it, this voice will be weak, underused, and inexperienced. Your self-awareness skills, like muscles, need training and practice. As you learn to challenge your assumptions and expand your understanding, you will become wiser. Instead of trying to find your inner guru, you will realize that self-awareness cannot simply be found. It must be educated. Here is yet another paradox: the voice that can guide you must, first, be guided *by* you. To lead the voices within, you first need to train your inner leader.

As the truth seeker within you learns and evolves, you will experience many transformations. While there is no universal rubric to measure progress in self-awareness, many voyagers on this path experience similar milestones. One common outcome is the ability to relate to more of the world. You will see more of what is there (not only what is immediately interesting to you). You will learn from different people (not only those who make you feel nice). You will find multiple lessons in a variety of experiences (even, and especially, the unpleasant ones). You will begin to influence other people in meaningful ways (instead of merely role-playing with them). You will embrace the beauty of confusion (instead of reflexively seeking certainty).

You will discover what it means to be your own best friend. You will learn to laugh at the stories you tell yourself and to hold each part of you with gentle compassion. You will begin to understand the difference between the pain of self-deceit and the pain of honest self-observation. You will learn to improve yourself without disrespecting who you are. You will learn to accept yourself without enabling your self-destructive habits. But most of all, you will learn to be patient with your unique process of learning and healing. Through self-understanding, you will discover the true meaning of self-love.

When you first begin honing your awareness skills, you might find it easier to observe others' unconscious patterns than to find your own. In such situations, you will face a choice: judgment or awareness. Will you criticize and correct other people's unconsciousness? Or will you gently pick up the clarity with which you can see others, hold it like a piece of fine crystal, and place it between yourself and your reflection, so that you may see yourself through it? Each time you choose awareness, you will find similarities and draw comparisons. You will discover yourself through every person you meet.

Over time, you will notice changes in how you react to people. When someone makes you angry, you will not lash out or shut down. You will wonder about the meanings of your emotions. When you feel envious of someone, you will not pity yourself or glorify him. You will seek out his talents within you. Like this, you will churn social comparison into self-discovery and celebration. Once others' accomplishments no longer threaten your self-concept, you can be happy for their successes.

Your mental versions of other people will become as diverse as reality itself. You will begin to treat them as such. You will not seek to save people or be saved by them. Thus, your relationships will become richer and deeper. You can support others without worrying that they will become dependent on you. You will try to act as you believe is right rather than blindly playing the roles expected of you. No matter how many people try to use you to complete their imbalances, you will remain free. And you will show them how it's done.

By reacting to others from a sense of inner balance, you will teach them about freedom—not by preaching about it but by giving out samples. Your mere existence will send out ripples of change into the world. The people around you will either start their own self-balancing journeys or exit your periphery. As you notice how you affect others, you will surrender two things: credit and control. No matter how much you nourish them, some people will neither thank you nor realize that you helped. And no matter how well you treat them, other people will not learn a thing from you. Thus, you will learn to focus on doing your best and leave others' reactions up to them.

When it comes to the teachers you follow and the books you read, you will begin trusting different people. While, before, you might have believed the advice of "perfect" gurus who claim to live atop the precipice of enlightenment, you will begin to question such claims. By observing your journey of continual reinvention, you will begin to trust those who speak of self-development as an endless path rather than a mountain to climb. You will feel drawn to people who are self-aware because you will relate to their translations of the world.

You will find new guides as well—sometimes in surprising forms. For example, one of my wisest teachers has been nature. The more I have noticed the perfect imperfections in each tree, each leaf, each flower, the more I have allowed myself to love my blemishes. From nature, I have learned to accept death, embrace confusion, and celebrate diversity. I have learned to approach myself with the same awestruck appreciation that I feel for the forest path.

You will find the world within you, and you will find yourself in the world—both inseparable from one another and inseparable from reality. With open eyes and an open mind, you can observe art, music, films, architecture, poetry. The more deeply you look at the creations of others, the more you will understand yourself. You might delve into new creative pursuits or revisit ones from your past. You might also develop new interests. I, for instance, fell in love with abstract expressionism. For most of my life, I had turned my nose up at this kind of art. To discover my latent passion for it, I had to look longer, deeper.

With every door you open, you will find yet another door. To this, you will grow not only accustomed but also welcoming. You will begin to understand what I have been saying all along: self-awareness is a way of life. It is not a fad. It is not a pill. It is not a cream you can apply to the rash on your heart. Self-awareness is like eating, breathing, sleeping. There will be no fireworks, no miracle transformation. Instead, you will experience a slow, conscious, and often painful unraveling of your highest potential. One day, you will see that this is more magical than any so-called magic potion.

The more you walk into the arms of direct experience, the more you will come to understand why this book alone can do so little for you. Written words are, at best, static fingers pointing to dynamic reality. We read an illuminating idea or inspirational quote. We beg to know "How?" But no one can answer this question for anyone else. Your "how" is not in any book. Your "how" will fill the pages of history as you create it. You will forge your path as you walk it. The more you experience this, the more you will see how useless, and even dangerous, this book can be. It can reinforce an already imbalanced conversation between theory and practice. Philosophizing about life does not replace living it. And the more you realize how much this book can never do, the more you will come to appreciate the small purpose it *can* serve: to show you the warmth of your inner fire and inspire you to keep it kindled.

One day, you might revisit the authorities and answers that once kept you small. A teenager may leave home after high school and return a few years later with newfound gratitude and understanding. So it goes with you and self-help. Your relationship to personal development might have been imbalanced: you as the unconfident learner and the experts as wise oracles with all the answers. When you return with self-aware eyes, you will see more clearly. You will find flaws in the theories you believed were perfect. You will find holes in the arguments you thought were bulletproof. You will find inconsistencies in each of your once-deified reference manuals. You will also find some pearls of wisdom in the books you threw aside. You will find yourself exploring viewpoints you once opposed and listening to opinions that disagree with your convictions. You will begin to entertain other people's ideas instead of picking a side and sticking to it. Imagine how creative you could be without always needing to define your boundaries. Imagine how much curiosity you could build without always needing to know where you stand.

You will discover all these things, and so much more. The world is a fascinating kaleidoscope of opportunities to observe, to listen, to explore. With your hand on the door, you are almost ready to leave me. We have stood here in this little shack on the edge of your wilderness for days, perhaps weeks. You've listened to me talk about your mysterious inner jungle. You have your compass. You have an understanding of potential dangers. But this is only the beginning. No matter how much I have tried to prepare you, preparation is not enough. You must explore.

Before I let you go, I want to mention one more thing: changing the world. Your journey might take you down the path of being a teacher, a leader, a healer. Not only by example but also by profession. Or you might choose to channel your awareness into art, business, or politics. Of course, this is not necessary. This idea might resonate with some part of you, or it might not. Plenty of wise, self-aware people have no books, no followers, and no biography; their lives are still meaningful and important.

If you do feel called to step into a leadership position, self-awareness will be your greatest asset. With inner balance, you will spread peace everywhere you go. You will look deeply instead of splashing near the surface. You will promote harmony in your words and actions. You will not compete with other leaders or compare to them. You will work together with others to make meaningful changes. You will not measure success in numbers: dollars, followers, ranks, sales, reviews, Facebook likes. Rather, you will measure by people helped, connections made, and moments savoured. You will help people accept themselves by being real with them. You will not show up on the pulpit for attention or approval. You will show up because you have something important to say. You will build tribes instead of cults. You will see your followers as equals. You will learn with them, and they will trust you. And there is nothing like the trust of people who resonate with your most authentic, vulnerable self to push you, every day, to do your best. It will hold you to a higher standard of behaviour.

As a self-aware leader, you can be honest. This is the missing element in so many ineffective and addictive doctrines. You can tell people the things that are true but hard to hear. Not everyone will be brave enough to sidestep idealism, but those who do will appreciate your honesty. If you do not describe the darkness and the light, the voyager who has followed in your footsteps will believe he is lost. He will blame himself or blame you for teaching him lies. By being honest about what the journey looks like—failures, warts, and all—your teachings will become sources of consolation rather than frustration. As that voyager travels down the crooked, lonely paths within him, he may find a dark, terrifying cave, but if you mentioned it, he will feel elated. Yes, he will think, it looks horrifying, but at least I'm on track if I've found this awful thing. Your honesty may be bitter medicine, but when it digests, it'll provide such potent healing that its taste will become a distant memory.

You will also formulate a healthier relationship to doubt. Instead of doubting yourself, you will doubt your ideas. Disbelief will guide you toward truth. A fanatic preaches not only to erase doubt within his followers but also to erase it within himself. A truth seeker, however, embraces doubt—not instead of faith but with it. She puts question marks around everything and encourages others to do so too. When her open mind finds some pattern again and again, she doesn't have to convince herself or anyone else that what she's found is important. At the end of the day, the greatest irony is this: when the truth seeker finds something to believe in, she believes it more fully than the fanatic ever could.

Now more than ever, we need truth seekers. So many people try to look happy while they die inside. So many businesses try to make things look beautiful for the consumer while, out back, the stench of garbage and corruption chokes the next generation. Then, we try to save ourselves like we try to save the planet. We swim in shallow waters. We craft beautiful surfaces and superficial solutions while decay spreads in the depths. Every time we push a mask over reality, it pushes back. Still, we keep pushing. We keep hiding.

Mary Catherine Bateson once said that because we do not see the "delicate interdependencies" all around us, we unknowingly break them. We cannot love something we don't understand. And our biggest misunderstanding is this: we keep trying to save the world, save ourselves. But we are not here to be heroes. We are here to learn, explore, wonder. We must give up salvation and take up understanding.

When we recognize ourselves as a part of nature, we start to care about nature's survival as much as we care about our own. When we perceive ourselves as members of a unified human race, we start to care about other people. When we embrace the world as an extension of ourselves, we start to love it. Thus, we start to care for it. We must seek to understand everything together, or we will love nothing at all. It takes courage. It takes trust. It takes curiosity.

I believe that everyone has an inner truth seeker, and I believe we can cultivate a culture that allows people to explore, educate, and use this voice in their daily lives. We can make self-awareness a norm. And it starts with each of us— with you and me. As you dig your teeth into your assumptions, your teeth become sharper. You can dig deeper. You become what the world needs simply by helping yourself. It's not easy, but it is worth it. The truth, as they say, hurts. But they also say it sets you free.

One thing is for sure—you will make mistakes. Learn to learn from them. Learn to forgive yourself. Learn to laugh when everything falls apart because, sometimes, it will. Your plans will be broken, and you will try to tell yourself stories about what "plans" and "broken" must mean for nothing unplanned to have happened. Remember that when things don't go according to plan, they go according to truth. No matter how painful the reality, it is reality nonetheless. There is dignity in facing the truth without trying to cut it down to a more manageable size. There is honour in acceptance. A truth seeker doesn't put spices on each moment before tasting it and thus knows reality's many flavours. Even the bitter. Even the sour.

So listen, watch, wonder. Relish the stars dancing in the sky above you. Let each moment show you who you are and why you are here. Stay humble. Stay open. And don't forget to laugh at yourself once in a while. No one will understand you, except the ones lying in the grass beside you, laughing at the same incomprehensible stars. And that, my friend, will be a life well lived.

How You Can Help
(The "Marketing Plan")

✴ ✴ ✴ ✴ ✴ ✴ ✴ ✴

In the book publishing industry, they ask, "What's your marketing plan?" Large publishing houses invest thousands of advertising dollars to drive books onto the bestseller charts. Driven by buzz, people buy the book, read the first chapter (if that), and then shelve it. By the next month, it's another book. I hope that *The Art of Talking to Yourself* can throw a wrench in not only traditional self-help models but also traditional book marketing methods.

This book doesn't have a marketing team or a publicist. My plan, instead, is to leave it up to you: the reader. I trust you. *You* are my marketing plan.

Do you think this book is important? If you do, then please help me spread its message. If you have downloaded this book or received it for free, I only ask that you pay special attention to what I am about to say. There are many ways to help without giving money. Here are some of them:

✴ Leave a review on as many book review platforms as you can. Some of these include Amazon, Barnes and Noble, and Goodreads. Amazon.com is by far the most influential, so it helps to post a review there in addition to your home base one (e.g. Amazon.ca, Amazon.co.uk).

- ✖ If you have a blog, post a recommendation or a review. If you sign up for an Amazon Associates account, you can make a small profit from your referral.

- ✖ Tell your friends and family about the book. Even better, get them copies as gifts.

- ✖ Go to your local library and, if they don't already have a copy, ask them to order some.

- ✖ Submit quotes from the book to quotes sites.

- ✖ Many social media platforms limit the exposure of inspirational pages to get them to pay for advertising. Thus, every time you interact with me on social media, it helps. This also applies to your favourite indie sites, authors, and books—help them out!

- ✖ If you listen to a podcast, vlog, TV show, or radio show that features relevant topics, ask if they can have me as a guest. This is what publicists do: they use their media connections to push authors onto various platforms. By making a request as a listener, you are not only helping spread this book's message, but you're also affecting the power structure of the media.

- ✖ Order through your local bookstore. Most stores do not order books without a publicist-led, nationwide marketing plan. The only way they make an exception is when enough customers request to order the book.

These are all the suggestions I have for you. I hope that this list has given you an idea of how you can support not only *The Art of Talking to Yourself* but also the authors, entrepreneurs, and leaders who choose to operate outside the outdated corporate systems that have too long controlled the way we consume information. Activism often tries to force companies to change what they supply to the public. I say, let us change what we, as consumers, demand. Then, the supply will change itself.

Thank you in advance for your help and support. I couldn't do this without you.

Love,

About the Author

Like every human being, Vironika Tugaleva is an ever-changing mystery. At the time of writing this, she was an award-winning author, life coach, and digital nomad. She spent her days writing, dancing, singing, running, doing yoga, going on adventures, and having long conversations. But that was then. Who knows what she's doing now? Keep up at www.vironika.org.